CULTURE AND DIFFERENCE

ESSAYS ON CANADIAN SOCIETY

Cheers,

Howard

ESSAY SERIES 54

Canada Council
for the Arts

Conseil des Arts
du Canada

ONTARIO ARTS COUNCIL
CONSEIL DES ARTS DE L'ONTARIO

Guernica Editions Inc. acknowledges the support of The Canada Council for the Arts.
Guernica Editions Inc. acknowledges the support of the Ontario Arts Council.
The Ontario Arts Council is an agency of the Government of Ontario.

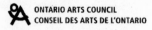

CULTURE
AND DIFFERENCE

ESSAYS ON CANADIAN SOCIETY

EDITED BY

HOWARD A. DOUGHTY

AND MARINO TUZI

GUERNICA

TORONTO – BUFFALO – LANCASTER (U.K.)
2011

Howard A. Doughty and Marino Tuzi, Guest Editors
Guernica Editions Inc.
P.O. Box 117, Station P, Toronto (ON), Canada M5S 2S6
2250 Military Road, Tonawanda, N.Y. 14150-6000 U.S.A.

Distributors:
University of Toronto Press Distribution,
5201 Dufferin Street, Toronto, (ON), Canada M3H 5T8
Gazelle Book Services, White Cross Mills, High Town, Lancaster LA1 1XS U.K.

Printed in Canada.
First edition.

Legal Deposit — Second Quarter
Library of Congress Catalog Card Number: 2007941179
Library and Archives Canada Cataloguing in Publication
Culture and difference : essays on Canadian society /
edited by Howard A. Doughty and Marino Tuzi.
(Essay series ; 54)
ISBN 978-1-55071-287-2
1. Canada—Civilization. 2. Canada—Intellectual life. 3. Canada—Social
conditions. I. Doughty, Howard A., 1945- II. Tuzi, Marino, 1952- III. Title.
IV. Series: Essay series (Toronto, Ont.) ; 54
FC95.5.C85 2008   306.0971   C2008-905975-1

CONTENTS

ACKNOWLEDGEMENTS

Culture and Difference is dedicated to the memory of Donald J. Weller (1946-1998) and of Will Griffis (1943-2001), two good teachers and two good friends.

The editors of this book of essays would like to acknowledge the invaluable support of Antonio D'Alfonso of Guernica Editions.

FOREWORD

MARINO TUZI

The America Revolution, or what some people consider a colonial mercantile rebellion against Great Britain, created two countries, the United States of America and the rest of British North America, which eventually would become Canada. The U.S.A. was the first "new nation" or independent state in the former British colonies in the Northern hemisphere. Since the American Revolution and after Confederation, many Canadian thinkers and academics have perceived or even conceptualized Canada as a non-American nation, wary of individualism and bound to British tradition. For much of their history, Canadians have exhibited a range of contradictory attitudes towards the U.S.A. Many Canadians have alternately and even simultaneously disparaged, distrusted, disdained, envied, imitated, praised, and adored their American neighbours. The relationship between Canada and the U.S.A. has been ambivalent and rather complex, incorporating affinities and irresolvable differences.

The political leaders who collaborated to create Canada belonged to two main cultural communities. One group was composed of French settlers and imperialist functionaries, who had emigrated from France from the seventeenth century to the eighteenth century, before the onset of the American

Revolution. They had established themselves on the North American continent and they were abandoned eventually by imperial France, after the French army's decisive defeat by the British military, years before the French Revolution, which ushered in a new regime and a radical political doctrine. The French people in Canada were called many names. They were perceived to be "conservative-minded" because of their allegiance to the Catholic Church, their respect for authority, and their belief in the importance of community. The other major group of settlers and colonial bureaucrats was comprised of people from various parts of the United Kingdom, many of whom had escaped from revolutionary America and had settled in southern Ontario, the eastern townships of what is modern Quebec, and the Maritime provinces. These British settlers and colonials hated the United States with the kind of passion that only unwilling emigrants can feel. Their loyalty to England and adherence to British tradition had set them apart from their fellow colonials in America. In British North America, these political émigrés, who were referred to as the United Empire Loyalists, supported "traditional conservatism," believing in the notion that collectivity transcended individualism.

In the nineteenth century, the established French and English communities absorbed newcomers from the United Kingdom who immigrated in search of a better life: there were indigent Scots crofters, impoverished Irish peasants, and poverty-stricken English people of various descriptions. Some of these people joined the conservative cause and entered politics. One of them, Sir John A. Macdonald, has been generally credited for the creation of Canadian nationhood. As such, he is also remembered for designing the "National Policy," one part of which was a national railway system linking the east to the west, the main purpose of which was to separate Canada economically from the U.S.A., ensuring its political sovereignty. Other Canadians became political radicals. In English Canada, one of these people, William Lyon Mackenzie, was blamed for being the main actor in the rebellion of 1837 in Upper Canada, which attempted to end British colonial rule. He is remembered for wanting to get rid of Tory corruption and to create a more democratic society, which was similar to the U.S.A., valuing free enterprise and individualism. He did not succeed in transforming the established order, which many of the United Empire Loyalists had helped to entrench in English Canada.

In the late nineteenth century, after Confederation, after the creation of Canadian nationhood, and to the present day, waves of immigrants have come to Canada. As a result, Canada has become a culturally and racially diverse society. There are many people from various ethnic origins, such as Ukrainian, German, Italian, Chinese, South Asian, Greek, Polish, and Caribbean. Many Canadians boast that Canada is the most "multicultural" and "multiracial" country in the world. It is commonly believed that Canada is a country in which ideological and cultural diversity ensures social and political stability.

Today, many people, from different cultural and social backgrounds, call themselves "traditional conservatives." Some of them are either inaccurate (such as those who proclaim the primacy of individualism and free enterprise) or else they are confused (such as those who support "social" or "moral" conservatism in reference to such areas as family, sexual orientation, and social justice).

In the past, traditional conservatism has been associated with some quite impressive people including Sir John A. Macdonald and, more recently, the philosopher George Grant, and the late political strategist and columnist Dalton Camp, who was an explicit advocate of "traditional con-

servatism" in his later years. To these people, the British
and European emphasis on tradition, memory, and social
order was not only critical in preserving Canada's cultural
distinctiveness, but it was fundamental to the egalitarian
nature of Canadian society. Tradition, memory, and social
order formed the basis for conceptualizing social justice. As
was the case for the majority of Canadians, "traditional
conservatives", who often tended ideologically to transcend political party lines, cared deeply about social justice.

Today, most of the publicly visible individuals, namely
academics, politicians, and business people, who call themselves "conservatives" have a point of view that is opposed
to traditional conservative ideas about justice and social
stability. Often, they choose novelty over tradition, technology over religion, republicanism over monarchy, liberty
over obligation, consumerism over citizenship, expediency
over commitment, assimilation over diversity, and the
unfettered rights of the individual over the harmony of the
community. Sometimes they call themselves "neo-conser-
vatives" and they may have an affinity with "neo-liberals,"
with a liberalism that supports corporate-consumerism and
has lost its sense of egalitarianism. For the past several
decades, these "new conservatives" have managed to succeed in defining the national political and social agenda.
They have put social services, primarily public health and
education, under great pressure, intensifying economic
inequality and damaging social stability. They have no criterion of value other than that based on the market place.
For them, anything, such as democracy or cultural diversity, can be turned into a commodity, divested of its ethical
and cultural substance. A famous conservative once said
that success is the only criterion of virtue for those individuals who are of vulgar judgement.

The essays in this book do not attempt consciously to represent or unambiguously endorse authentic conservative values, but they do reflect the spirit of traditional conservatism, which made it possible for Canadians to enjoy a measure of ideological and cultural diversity not commonly available in the United States. This book demonstrates efforts to manifest and support such diversity, aiming for a better understanding of what makes Canada a unique country even today.

If there is a recurrent message that is transmitted by the essays in this book, it is that cultural and social experience in Canada is often marked by a cultural perspective that does not emanate from what one may call a purely English or French context. Yet this "ethnic" or "minority" perspective is shaped by and has evolved with various, complex, contradictory, and unstable elements of mainstream English Canadian and Quebecois culture. In this book of essays, minority experience underlies different aspects of contemporary Canadian society, namely the mass media, literature, politics, the Canadian Constitution, and economics.

In his or her own way, each writer suggests or implies that the connection and interplay between "minority group" and "majority culture" has affected the manner in which a particular segment of Canadian social reality has been constructed. Each writer intimates that history and ideology have structured the ways in which individuals perceive significant and current cultural and political events in Canada. The essays of the writers in this book attempt to challenge the reader to reconsider specific and established cultural and social givens. At the same time, the essays provide an alternative reading of what constitutes many aspects of modern Canadian society.

LITERARY AND CULTURAL STUDIES

READING DISPLACED WRITING

Replacing the Context, Affirming the Transient

WILLIAM ANSELMI

In a recent interview about Roberto Benigni's *La vita è bella*, the German philosopher, Rüdiger Safranski, defines the aesthetic process succinctly with: "Ogni processo estetico è sempre la trasfigurazione di un evento tragico o anche orribile in una forma che comunichi piacere a chi la guarda."[1] Basically, an aesthetic process is the transfiguration of a tragic or horrible event in a form that communicates pleasure to the one that is watching.

Although various works dealing with a writing-without-power-allocation have appeared in recent years, what is often considered "minority" or "ethnic" or "marginal" and for our purpose "displaced" writing seems to lack not only a proper pressmark, but an aesthetic that would grant it an independent status. Such is the case for Italian Canadian writing, a writing which is formulaically ascribed to the *elsewhere within*, given the neutralizing polarization between the governmental policies of Multiculturalism and Biculturalism.

By the "elsewhere within" what is meant is the presence in our lifeworld of the *different*, the Other from the historical subject of the dominant discourse. Elsewhere, I have used the formulation of "dominant discourses" – in keeping with a redefinition of Canadian power structures –

for, what is more appropriately, the pervasive discourse of "two dominant minorities." In other words, by analyzing the ethnocultural lifeworld that inhabits the Canadian-scape, we will see that the two dominant discourse structures do not represent themselves as ethnocultural components. In a previous work, Kosta Gouliamos and I have identified this occurrence as the political need to re-ethnicize these two ethnocultural components in order to break away from the hierarchical model of Settlers vs. Ethnics (or, Founding Fathers vs. Illegitimate Children), so as to bring about participation in the emancipatory model of a "nomadic transcultural federation."[2]

The implication of this working model is obviously to politically and socially reconfigure the marginalized participation of the phantasmagorical, multicultural "dominant" group. That is, the sum of Canadian ethnocultural groups that have been continuously displaced, not only from the space of origin but from history and authentic social presence as well. In this sense, an aesthetic of displaced writing is also the postulate of reoccupied space of transient belonging. Certainly, unlike the representative of economic Darwinism, the corporations' transnational behaviouristic model or Transnational Being (TB for short), the single ethnocultural subjectivity cannot invoke for himself/herself but a precarious statehood/citizenship in the form of passive reification, rather than the historical affirmation of the nomadic experience.

It will become clear in our next section why the point of departure for an aesthetic of displaced writing is also to be found in what formulates its marginalization. To find, that is, in the everyday *praxis* of endemic subaltern modalization, the Safranskian lifeworld event that, paradoxically, reinforces displacement as a privileged communicative heterogeneity.

Exemplary marginalizations: The under siege mentality

Diane Francis, the columnist in the "Financial Post" section of *The National Post*, has been able to surpass Homer's (however disputed) wordy construction of the world. Her mimetic renditions of the *Iliad* and the *Odyssey*, the complementary writings that depict – through the metaphor of a siege, *the conquering stasis* and of a return, *the wandering back movement* – the whole of the ancient world, its *afflato* (inspiration, afflatus) is to be found in two, definitive, articles. With the *Edmonton Journal* acting as the affiliated host, between the 24th of January 1999 ("Sanctity of Canada's border criminally compromised – Immigration needs strong dose of reality") and the 14th of March 1999 ("Immigration sponsorship policy a disaster – $1B annual bill for taxpayers as relatives opt out"), Francis becomes Canada's celebrated, blind poet. Perhaps, it is worth paraphrasing one of Emile Cioran's aphorisms in that *every thought is derived by a sensation that we have hindered* to fully appreciate Francis' poetics of exclusionary practice (PEP), or the rhetoric of AIDS (Anti-Immigration and Defamation Strain).

Francis' discourse could be the official TCE (Transnational Canadian Enunciation), that is the mediatic representation of the dominant political economy. As such, it works to domesticate and neutralize the "different" in Canada by resorting to pseudo-class structure differentiation, while collapsing the ethnic element into a controllable economic category. This process becomes the highpoint of moving into the new millennium. As a process that is now overtly manifest, it is a presence that is implicit in polarizing ethnicity as subaltern commodity to Canadian pre/post identity formation paradigms. Given this status of affairs, the necessity of state hegemony and the survival of nine-teenth-century practices of social control make it possible for strict hygienic representation of the lifeworld.

There does not seem to be a need anymore for, (a) the "dominant minorities" to have a conceptual framework for practicing racism, since it has reached what is a useful saturation point, and therefore (b) it is now necessary to displace racism into the ethnocultural groups themselves which constitute the "majority-reality" of Canada. In so doing, the commentaries by Francis have a precise target audience, which we would better identify with the more familiar ethnic groups, than with lonesome WPE (White Power Elites).

In terms of subjugating one's self to a theory of "belonging" to the racially administered reality of the dominant minorities, economic class status is the key. That is, belonging passes through a refining process, the acquisition of a special skill: *hara-kiri*, the art of becoming one's own enemy, a specific species for an autoimmunization disease. The process is mitigated, edulcorated by investing one's self with the pretense of participaction; a tacky tachism by which belonging is performance, hygienically enacted, as a dominant minority, yet without socio-political power. This titillating Eldorado is then the mirage created by the media: the expulsion out of one's self of the different though can never be a guarantee of permanence, of legitimacy as a citizen.

Manifest destiny, primary part: The sanitized anomaly

The title "Sanctity of Canada's border criminally compromised" posits a stupendous linguistic construction within a defining context. The alliteration is already a promise of a

subtle and refined poetics, while at the same time present-
ing what is not right in Canada (pun intended). But, we still
need to define what constitutes the "criminally compromised." So far, we have the religious domain invoked for
Nationhood, Canada akin to Godhead; its "sanctity" – the
preservation of its holiness, its unspoiled hygienic entity –
is called into play. But, problematically, a defiling process is
at work: the "border" of its existence is, already, under
unlawful penetration. The culprit is not far away since
"Immigration needs a strong dose of reality" seems to refer
to the immigrant matrix; and, the control system operated
upon it is envisioned as absent, or better, as an actually dis-
eased control system: "dose of reality" refers to a medical
terminology shifted into a jocular understatement. So far,
immigration is seen as introducing a malady into this holy
space, a space which must be "reclaimed" for the new millennium.

Francis establishes a *praxis* for the recuperation of the
lost true religion in her commentary. Through the apparent
subterfuge of a critical reading of the way refugees are
allowed in Canada, the way 5000, who have been ordered
deported, have disappeared into invisibility, the immigrant
paradigm is called into question and finally delegitimized.
Definitions for refugees/immigrants abound: "Officials
take the word of the *undesirable* that they will voluntarily
return to be kicked out. Predictably, these *sleazes* disappear
into the *muck* they came from and end up doing burglar-
ies, muggings, prostitution or defrauding banks or welfare
offices to make ends meet" (italics mine).[3]

Not because the *National Post* defines itself as the only
Canadian paper – one that transcends the regional/munici-
pal status and claims national representation (beyond the
Toronto-the-Good-based *Globe and Mail*) – that one can
ask the following rhetorical question: what manipulative

ideological schemata is at work in the discourse? In other words, once my own status as an immigrant and then Canadian (whatever it might mean in this artificial world) has been defined as: (1) undesirable, (2) sleaze and finally, so far, (3) muck, what I am left with is: am I (second rhetorical question) a virus contaminating and endangering the sanctity of the space I live in?

For an immigrant to be *undesirable,* there must exist a text spelling out the characteristics of desirability (work policies notwithstanding). As a *sleaze*, after having consulted the *Gage Canadian Dictionary*, the immigrant is poor and flimsy: (again, [1] light and thin; frail [2] not serious or convincing, inadequate) thus, a person such as myself would be genetically unfit, as you can see, not serious or convincing (the word "inadequate" is too suggestive of another plane of discourse for me to go there). Now, *muck* is quite troublesome, indicating an unhealthy mixture of "mud and other things." Back to the Canadian dictionary, which gives in the main usage: (1) dirt, filth; (2) anything filthy, dirty or disgusting; (3) moist farmyard manure; (4) well-decomposed peat, used in manure.

Francis correctly goes on to depict the refugee/ immigrant reason for being: "Others, disinclined to break laws that overtly, disappear into their communities, working illegally in sweatshops populated by illegal aliens like themselves, contributing absolutely nothing to this country except babies."[3] The characterization of an impossibility of recognition of the different, given their other-sameness, is also indicative of an explosive reproduction mode. It is an alarm that the West has often sounded in its control-compass: West versus East and North versus South. By allocating to Canada a one-in-seven status, as far as industrialization goes, this ideal mapping out of wished for hygienic representations is cohesive with a CPMS (Capitalistic

PostModern Society), the everyday mediatic practices of subjugation and removal.

As far as fear and control mechanisms are concerned, the best passage is in the ending paragraph of the third. In reference to Canada allowing people to sneak in under false pretenses, Francis goes on to say that: "One Nigerian who snuck in this way explained he did not lie at the border as to his intention to declare refugee status. He told a hearing that a witch doctor gave him a potion that made him invisible, cut him into seven pieces and smuggled him into Canada."[4]

Semiotically, the oppositional framework between "the true religious foundation of the West" and "superstitious third world mechanism" is well presented by the *Financial Post* columnist. By the same token, the cohesiveness of the text is reinforced by the way Francis is able to invoke a poetics of refined racism for third world dwarfs, by the opportune internal rhyming scheme: "muck"/"snuck," which is also reinforced by a colour-coded referentiality, a special isotopy. Finally, this article makes one last, special claim for legitimized belonging, which must be quoted fully: "Retroactive action should be taken to turf out the *rubbish* that has been allowed in. Police computers could find the identity of all immigrants or refugees who have ever been convicted of committing a serious crime. If they have, *they should be asked to leave immediately even if they have become a citizen*"[5] (Italics mine).

Here then is the ultimate question set: Who belongs in Canada? How do you stay Canadian? Is it a question of temporality? Are some Canadians more Canadian than others? If the immigrant subject is able to internalize this discourse, and now schizoid in the practice of belonging and self-destruction, will he/she finally belong?

Secondary partitions: Tracing the malady

In its second commentary, "Immigration sponsorship poli-cy a disaster – $1B annual bill for taxpayers as relatives opt out," the attack on Canadian immigration laws and offi-cials continues undisturbed. Actually, if in the first article the reader was presented with a call to self-destruction, the implosion of the immigrant ethnocultural problematic, now we have the possibility to trace the roots of such a problem: "An estimated 6,000 (welfare) cases are immi-grants receiving social assistance because of sponsorship breakdown."[6] Could it be that, as it has been said: ". . . the dominant system deliberately chooses disorders such as anxiety, panic, phobias and fear as vital components of socio-political or cultural learning and communication pat-terns?"[7] Invoking by the constructed reality of scapegoat-ing the ethnic, attributing to the different not economic contribution but subtraction, is it not the redundant tech-nique of social hegemony achieved through fear?

Tenuous affirmations using pseudo-fact statements – numbers being objective – can then lead to the normalizing text without a glitch: "It's a racket is what it is and mostly about people defrauding the immigration system to get rel-atives who aren't appropriate for this country inside this country."[8] The key word is *appropriate*, taking on a defi-nite resonance when we connect it to the questions elicited in the previous commentary. A final answer is given by Francis:

> But taxes are already ruinously high and social spending should be restricted to looking after Canadians. Immigration should be restricted to the able-bodied and those with marketable skills that can make a contribution to Canada. Not cost it precious tax dollars needlessly.[9]

Obviously, notwithstanding the contradictions in the two cultural formation texts, it must be pointed out that immigrants do pay taxes. If it seems a trivialization of the immigrant experience, nevertheless it is something which in the polarized Francisian vision of Canadians vs. Immigrants, must be completely spelled out.

Finally, in the comparison of the two commentaries, there is no need to establish what is being invoked: it is not just the proper immigrant, but the need for special rules for the maintenance of the desirable, appropriate ethnoculturalities. As the recuperation of the immigrant goes – Who is not an immigrant? – a special category is set up with the stress on historical settlers, those who must have founded this nation. In other words, what is offered is the historical rewrite of Canadian reality by a filtering process of its past and future, in order to maintain its present in Kapitalism's eternal presence. Perhaps, the following passage from *Elusive Margins*, will clarify the issue:

> Thus, a particular manipulation is manifested in the nomadic experience, one where history is denied and/or rewritten in favour of capital's cannibalization of the subject's consciousness through a nostalgia for the future. More precisely, this nostalgia for the future entails a reductive process where history becomes a commodity. The present is excluded since it becomes an eternal present; the past is banalized according to the precepts of mass media practices such as advertising, fashion magazines, instant news books, museums, etc. With the abolition, or the complete realization of the time frame of linearity, the future is envisioned as that which moves out of present alienated conditions. Progress ultimately becomes defined according to a nostalgia for the future which entails the millenarian discourse. This pseudo-mythical quality of capital gives rise to the indefinite postponement of self-realization. The schizophrenic subject is reduced to imaginary/illusory identity and a created participation in consumeristic rituals.[10]

Rewriting the immigrant: Disciplinaction

Who defines what is displaced, or immigrant writing? The question arises immediately if we are to put into context the cultural and social implication of such a statement. For a definition of immigrant writing must take into account the relations of power that govern such a construct. Its context is such that immigrant writing is not a neutral term but becomes the writing that is not mainstream Canadiana – not a writing which partakes of an implicit definition of belonging.

Writing belongs within a realm of power relations: who gets published, who gets recognized, and whoever decides upon the parameters, the canon by which a writing is inscribed within a system of governance and legitimacy. Once again, putting into a framework of analysis such a statement must elicit the political and cultural arenas. Therefore, if the context, by necessity is the Canadian writescape, what can immigrant writing be? It is a question, which must be asked, if we are to make sense of such a statement and void tacit sub-servience: immigrant writing becomes by definition that which does not belong within a stable, normative system. Everything else outside the space of immigration is belonging, that is we must call into question the code of historicity if we are to claim space for such a position.

Belonging is the self-fulfilling act, the act of appropriating one's self in a normative sense. By establishing one's territorial *praxis*, everything outside of it is precisely the outer limits. Once again, who belongs? Those who claim history and write it out belong, because by so doing they establish the cultural mode of interpretation and detection, establishing the boundary line of visibility and exclusion. As Raymond Samuels II tells us in his *National Identity in Canada and Cosmopolitan Community*:

> Canada becomes a vertically arranged society, of benign apartheid, characterized by its non-American North-Americanness. Governance becomes a process of mediating status anxieties, brought by those in the polity seeking to defend, or to revise their status . . . The idea of the "founding races," helps to promote the perpetuation of "Canada" as a status-oriented society based on a colonial compact.[11]

How is immigrancy to legitimate its belonging? It is not a case of adhering to established paradigms of self-hate and devaluation in favour of reproducing stereotypes for the sake of economic interests. Rather, it is the process of internalization of our, ironically despicable, static quadruple identities (that which I was, that which I am now, that which I never was, that which I could have been). In what sense despicable? Different subjectivity is embedded into a neocolonial mindset, a double colonized lifeworld. Our particular experience of immigration has led us to be colonized both by the host country and by the country of provenance. The resistance to immigrant writing – one of ongoing identity making processes – by the Canadian mainstream and Italian academia is a case in point. What is then this source of discomfort that afflicts us? We define ourselves by the cultural milieu that we inhabit. But, and this is precisely the main point, those particular objects, those texts, artistic and cultural, which could help situate us in the identity-making process are, because of their not being categorically here-or-there, denied or recuperated in such a form (for example Nino Ricci's Governor General's Award) which confirms the stereotype. For this, immigrant writing is treated as the writing of appeasement, that is a writing of limited sociological interest. We pretend, somehow, to forge identities based on cultural materiality, which has little relevance to identity shoppers coming from an

Italian Canadian background. In other words, in our colonized minds we seem to refer back to an absolute (*negative nostalgia*) or be confronted by a crypto-absolute (*displacement continuity*), but we cannot ever refer to the dynamics of the lifeworld in the space of identity-formation processes. This failure in acknowledging our immediate presence makes us prisoners of a process of polarization without escape, the doubly (neo)colonized mind.

Yet, in this process of coming to terms with immigrant writing we must not forget that it is precisely the existence of Italian academia that, paradoxically, fosters it. Immigrant writing, by its diasporic nature, is also a process of ongoing distantiation: being neither here nor there ontologically. It is a writing, at its best, questioning not only the space of arrival but also the departure space, as is the case with Caterina Edwards' *The Lion's Mouth* of confronting the cultures of oppression and pseudo-sustenance, cosmetic histories, phantasmagorical representations. Within this dialectical space, between what can be called *la dominanza del recupero* (dominance of recuperation) and *il recupero della servitù* (recuperation of servitude) displaced writing defines itself as other-than; hence, the necessity of a strong Italian academic presence. Simply said, it offsets at best the immediate assimilation process bestowed upon the second and other generations. Thus, in this context, a Fiorella De Luca Calce community-construction has more to offer than a linear, feminist reading of Italian Canadian reality in her first novel *Toni*. We must not forget that appropriation-towards-assimilation, through a reductive modalization, exists and manifests itself at all levels. Let us make a case in point, while critically delving in recent history: the attack against the teaching of languages in post-secondary education.

Carleton University, in Ottawa, has been foregrounded

as the *avant-garde* process – 1997 – of the elimination of languages and literatures other than English or French. Defamation was used as the common practice in the public space, as was the case with the November editorial in *The Citizen* that addresses this problem. The issue of closing SLLCLS (School of Language and Literatures and Comparative Literary Studies: Classics, German, Italian, Russian, Spanish and Comparative Literary Studies) was supported by this solid reason: the closure of "mediocre programs" given by "poorly trained people." That set the agenda for misinformation, financial mistakes worth $500,000, and the intentional use of fear as psychological warfare.

What is important overall about Carleton's situation has various levels of reading: this process, the physical elimination of the languages programme (German, Italian, Russian and Spanish) is not a local thing (act locally, think globally). It is the real, concrete, actual reality of a successful attack in Ontario, and valid for the rest of Canada as well, against space and lives. An attack against differences for the solidification of the neocolonial *praxis* of punishment and exclusion. Having had success, it is the beginning of a domino effect of closures. Canada is moving rabidly towards a politics of redefinition of the liberal Canadianscape, of removing whatever positive value Multiculturalism has provided as a governmental policy.

An apocalyptic wish to bring to closure differential experience seems to agitate the socio-cultural landscape. John O'Sullivan's recent Keith Joseph Memorial lecture is a case in point. In the abridged version offered the public by the *National Post*, what comes under attack is precisely our polyphonic existence. The title contains *in nuce* the ideological framing of removal, much like Francis' categorical operation. For, as we have in the title: "Is multiculturalism the next big anti-democratic idea? – The idea that a common culture oppresses minorities denies the possibility of a national community," a model of exclusion legitimizes and is legitimized by Francis' totalizing position. At this point it would be too easy to classify such practices as the natural exposition of a paper's ideological position and to dismiss them as rhetorical exercises. Rather, these commentaries/articles can be interpreted as the natural development of an ongoing reaction within the global discourse of oppression and marginalization – after all, the *National Post* is the virtual Canadian unifying voice. So that a statement such as: "Insofar as it has an impact on politics, multiculturalism systematically undermines the institutions of liberal democracy"[12] has precise consequences. How does multiculturalism undermine liberal democracy? O'Sullivan gives three basic reasons:

> By denying the legitimacy of the nation state, it undermines the only polity in which democracy flourishes . . . By asserting that a national common culture is oppressive to minorities, it denies the possibility of a national community . . . by declaring majority rule obsolete, it not only attacks the central idea of liberal democracy, but it does so on the spurious grounds that minorities are doomed to be perpetually out of power.[13]

Of course, the subtext is quite simply a call to arms to defend: God, Family and Country under the barbarian attack. Rehearsing on the fundamental malady of multiculturalism is an easy task as we move into the construction of a new millennium. What is been promoted is the negation of the ethnocultural component in favour of the continuous power exercises of "minority dominance" in Canada. The particularity of this piece is twofold: on one level it claims "liberal democracy" as the sole legitimate form of coexistence and expression, creating an incontestable absolute; on the other level it negates, by implication, that diversity can operate within a democratic structure, an old imperialistic framework of control. Of course, there are critical texts that can show the vacuous absolutist construct for what it is. What else but the tenant of an "end of history" ideology serving the interest of a shifting metaphor for Kapital's structure, be it a window on "New World order," "globalization" or simply on the micro level, soft personifications such as Bill Gates.

Pierre Clastres' *La société contre l'état*, or Fredy Perlman's *Against His-story Against Leviathan* do point to non-hierarchical social structures, non-absolutist power relations which have existed in the past and have formed a collective reservoir of practical direct democratic knowledge and *praxis* against erasure from His-story.[14] Elias Canetti, in his in-depth work *Masse und Macht*, has also shown the underlining principles of authoritarian socio-economic control, which has systematically oppressed human life.

It will not be sufficient to identify O'Sullivan's PWE reality, since linguistic manipulation is its core expression. A linguistic practice such as the one given above must be confronted at the outset, at the risk of entering into its polarizing game. When a statement such as "multiculturalist theories, though dressed in progressive language, are deeply reactionary"[15] the ludic is not the winning element, rather the derivative of the intentional manipulation of linguistic facts. This technique, of ascribing to the opponent the exact opposite linguistic characterization is the subterfuge by which dialectics is erased from democratic dialogue. Deeply irrational, while maintaining the facade of a critical discourse, this form of manipulation is entirely embedded in neo-fascistic practices of exclusion. Basically, we are witnesses, culturally and socially, to a (blocked) passage in time where not a paradigm shift, but a lifeworld shift has occurred.

Journalism, journalism

At this point, it is quite clear that the attempt of formulating an aesthetic of displaced writing must continuously take into consideration the contextual premises of our displaced subjectivities. They are to be found in the everyday experience of reality forming mechanisms, in loci of power, which have little to do with academic treatises if not in terms of providing an abundant materiality. Parameters, loci of power, mechanisms of control point to one revolving absolute context: the mediatic circle. The way personal identities are formed, cultivated and directed towards unattainable goals and happiness, procures a grammar of sublimation of our totality (potential and practical) of human experience. Fragmentation, isolation, disempowerment take the form of *naturalized* categorizations – self-interest, egotism, individualistic – normalized in our role as consuming and consumed agents. The mediatic circle: the array of communicative instruments constituted by CDs, television, radio, computer, cinema, etc., posit the consumer as its passive, zombied reflection while claiming in liberal democracy style its centrality in the process.

What has been foregrounded in this study though, is the newspaper text as opposed to other exemplar since, in a personal biased position a) the written word has still a solidity, a presence that zapped images cannot invoke, b) skepticism is a natural instrument as far as "globalizing" statements are concerned, such as the invocation of a national discursive entity on paper, and c) as a record, the journalistic text is still reflective of a dimension that other transient vitalities cannot claim, that of a social contract.

Nomadism, displacement, emancipatory practices

Francesco Loriggio, in his critical preface to *L'Altra Storia*, the first anthology of Italian Canadian writers to be published (original text with translation) in Italy, writing about the critical status of ethnic writing, has this to say:

> Emigrazione e immigrazione, insomma, aprono per la letteratura e per la critica letteraria una dimensione al di là dell'apparato concettuale tradizionale. Reintroducono nel dibattito il fattore sociale, ma con varie aggiunte, varie nuove clausole . . . Tanto per illustrare, il doppio *decalage* degli emigranti, la loro distanza spazio-temporale dall'Italia può essere intesa come un solco, un ritardo irrimediabile, oppure può essere concepita come un vantaggio ermeneutico . . . la temperie più facilmente riconoscibile della modernità.[16]

Emigration and immigration open up a new conceptual framework for literary criticism, one that must take into account the double *decalage* of the immigrants – their distance from and shifting Other perspective of the place of origin in their transition. On one hand we have a frozen time construct which continuously feeds on itself and seems to reflect, at another time interval, our postmodern reality of absolute time (the "tiny bubbles" construct). On the other, precisely because of the out-of-phase time construct, we have a modern hermeneutic vantage point (deep subjectivity).

In another work, I have pointed out the point of collusion between the Italian neo-*avant-garde* and displaced writing in general: while the neo-*avant-garde* has as its critical point of arrival the displacing of the historic alienated subject for a recuperation of its totality through experimental linguistic practices, displaced writing has as a starting point precisely the proclivity of the subject-in-belonging: material displacement. The aesthetic dimension, which is yet to be claimed by displaced writing in general, has as its context the discursive and representational exclusion previously analyzed (the Francisian world), and as its critical advantage the identity-doubling of its manifestation. In *Elusive Margins*, we have developed what should be called the static model of displaced identity as is given by the following graph.[17]

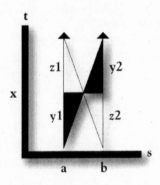

It was previously foregrounded ironically as despicable since the static model offers a quadruple identity: that which I was (y1), that which I am now (y2), that which I never was (z2), that which I could have been (z1). Starting with this model, I would like to add the dynamic model of identity representation, which shows beyond any doubt the postmodern ambivalence, since displacement necessarily entails the polyphonic reality of the nomadic experience. The dynamic model does not present a quadrupling anymore. It presents an open exponential system, since it calls for the mapping of any return/return movement. For example, in Caterina Edwards' *Lion's Mouth* the main character,

Bianca, returns three times to Canada from Italy that would mean a combination of twelve identity-postulates. Obviously, displaced writing is not legitimized quantitatively; the number of contents for the identity-formation paradigm present in nomadic reality is there to confirm the multiple content-aspects of the process.

The aesthetic included

Finally, the construction of an aesthetic of displaced writing is not an absolute model; it cannot entrench itself in such a modus operandi, since its very existence is limited in time. It is a transient and tensional model, that necessarily partakes of the critical changes in the evaluation of the artistic text in so far as those changes reflect perspectives of the object, rather than resorting to a limiting dominant canonization contextually bound.

Briefly, we have identified two aspects in its construction. One posits the context, in this case the *praxis* of marginalization/exclusion within the Canadian socio-culturescape. The displaced text is not a reaction to this antagonistic reality; rather it is brought under discriminatory scrutiny as an oppressive reaction to its own existence. Hence, the various formulations which deny it an aesthetic existence, and reduce its stature to sociological statements rather than poiesis, the artistic capability of ethnocultural self-representation and self-reflexivity. The second aspect takes into consideration the way displaced writing precedes postmodernity in terms of its natural polyphonic dimension, as well as representing the artistic departing point which neo-*avant-garde praxis* envisions as its final goal in the liberation of the subject from reification and alienation. The third aspect must necessarily deal with the question of authenticity, which can be defined as the critical ability of self-representation outside of formulaic or stereotypical canonizations. In other words, an aesthetic of displaced writing must take into account a possible combination of:

- the artistic text's political placement on the cultural map of power relations;
- its ability to represent the de-alienating, de-reifying potential inscribed in its existence;
- its endemic polyphonic nature as a representational mode;
- its ability to unmask stereotypical formations which are overtly or covertly ascribed to its existence;
- its syntactic and semantic manipulation of the language used – its distancing itself from standardized renditions;
- its propensity to challenge, manipulate and turn upside down/inside out representational expectations by part of the reader;
- its intertextual characteristics which might draw from and redefine textual representation of the departing and host culture.

These seven theses for the construction of an aesthetic system are not conceived as a complete system – they are part, instead, of a particular critical sensibility towards the affirmation of an inclusive, heterogeneous lifeworld.

NOTES

1. Rüdiger Safranski, interview with Stefano Vastano, "L'uomo che sdoganò l'Olocausto," *L'Espresso* (4 March, 1999), p. 134.
2. W. Anselmi and K. Gouliamos, *Elusive Margins: Consuming Media, Ethnicity, and Culture* (Toronto: Guernica, 1998).
3. Diane Francis, "Sanctity of Canada's border criminally compromised," *Edmonton Journal* (24 January, 1999).
4. *Ibid.*
5. *Ibid.*
6. *Ibid.*
7. Diane Francis, "Immigration sponsorship policy a disaster – $1B annual bill for taxpayers as relatives opt out," commentary in the *Edmonton Journal* (14 March, 1999).
8. Anselmi and Gouliamos, *op. cit.*, p. 124.
9. Diane Francis, "Immigration sponsorship policy a disaster."
10. *Ibid.*
11. Anselmi and Gouliamos, *op. cit.*, p. 15.
12. Raymond Samuels II, *National Identity in Canada and Cosmopolitan Community* (Ottawa: The Agora Cosmopolitan, 1997), p. 89.
13. John O'Sullivan, "Is multiculturalism the next big anti-democratic idea? The idea that a common culture oppresses minorities denies the possibility of a national community," *National Post*, 17 March, 1999.
14. *Ibid.*
15. *Ibid.*
16. Francesco Loriggio, "Introduzione," in F. Loriggio, ed., *L'Altra Storia* (Monteleone, Vibo Valentia, 1998), pp. 9-10.
17. Anselmi and Gouliamos, *loc. cit.*

GENDER AND ITS REPRESENTATION IN CANADIAN MINORITY LITERATURE

MARINO TUZI

It is argued that conventional gender roles are not natural, but socially and culturally scripted. "Sexual categories," observes Diana Fuss, "are no more and no less than social constructions, subject-positions subject to change and to historical evolution."[1] Elsewhere Toril Moi alludes to the idea that gender identities come out of "actual social [and] political structures" and these structures "produce . . . a homologous relationship between the subjective and the social."[2] Social relations are enacted and sustained by an underlying system of beliefs that is deeply politicized. What is presented as commonsensical in our understanding of gender roles and gender related behaviour is really based on ideological assumptions. Terry Eagleton notes that ideology often passes itself off as truth and as a disinterested aspect of human experience: "The largely concealed structure of values which informs and underlies our factual statements is part of what is meant by 'ideology.' By 'ideology' I mean, roughly, the ways in which what we say and believe connects with the power structure and power relations of the society we live in."[3] Ideological assumptions about the gendered subject are not just "the deeply entrenched, often unconscious beliefs which people hold." Ideology involves "those modes of feeling, valuing, perceiving and believing which have some kind of relation to the maintenance and reproduction of social power."[4] These beliefs and the attitudes that they generate "are by no means merely private quirks."[5] Contained by a largely patriarchal ideological system, "the feminine is at once constructed within the symbolic order, like any gender, and yet is relegated to its margins, judged inferior to masculine power. The woman is both 'inside' and 'outside' male society, both a romantically idealized member of it and a victimized outcast."[6]

This social reality is manifested in literature, revealing an underlying set of discontinuities and contradictions about gender. Fictional texts do not mechanically reproduce widespread cultural values and social ideologies. They are actively involved in interpreting the meanings of these values and ideologies and in working out new ideas to redefine the existing social system. Nevertheless, at some level of their activity, fictional texts are influenced by encompassing ideological forces to which they remain connected and also resist. There is a tension in literary texts between their questioning of prevailing attitudes and their support of them through their positioning within powerful social and cultural beliefs. The discrepancy is made obvious through the manner in which gender is fictionally represented. The contradictory actions of this fiction do not necessarily diminish the potency of ideological notions about gender, which are in circulation in a given social order.

Although there are many ways that a writer can picture masculinity and femininity, these representations operate in relation and in response to established social practices. The valorization of traditional femininity, in terms of the domestic and nurturing role of the woman in the minority Canadian communities, attempts to recover and legitimize women's history and experience in a patriarchal social system. Yet, this idealization reinforces the very male-based ideological assumptions about femininity, which it appears to be challenging. Similarly the evoking of femininity within a public sphere, particularly in a professional and capitalist context, is highly problematic since it is inclined to reproduce male-based ideas about social relations. This kind of representation tends to devalue feminine qualities, which have been traditionally associated with a woman's domestic role. It does so by emphasizing a competitive and consumer mindset that is shown to be preferable to women's conventionalized work as nurturers.

Aside from the issue of appropriation of voice, which is related to power relations in the marketplace and the process of cultural production, there is a tendency for male minority writers to depict women's experiences in a manner that is different from the representations of women by female minority writers. The placement of female minority writers in patriarchal society diverges in various degrees from that of their male counterparts. In representational terms, "maleness" frequently inserts itself in the construction of femininity in men's writing, despite the appearance that a given text is exploring gender from a woman's perspective.

In contrast to this male filtered view of female experience, minority women's writing examines the incongruities, ambiguities, and instabilities that underlie women's diverse positionings in the ethnic community and English Canadian society. Contradiction and ambiguity in minority women's writing, while they keep before the reader the inescapable connections to patriarchy, function within the context of a feminine consciousness of the world. In current women's writing, it is not simply a question of choosing between the private and the public sphere.

The focus here is not so much on the tasks related to the role that is performed but on the qualities and elements, which are associated with the given role. The splitting of the personal from the public sphere, which is itself a product of a patriarchal view of femininity, is resisted by women writers. In their fictional texts, the creative forces of femininity continually extend into various areas of activity, whether it is mothering, the pursuit of a professional career, or even artistic involvement.

The conjoining of the intimate and the social is reflected in literary texts, which are at once autobiographical accounts and particular interpretations of femininity and social reality. The books of fiction "are 'private' because they are wrought out of personal and often unconscious emotion and 'fictional' because the experiences have been transformed into the discourse of art. As invented worlds which reinvent and reshape reality, they offer new possibilities and new perspectives."[7] Both in daily life and in the realm of fiction, the subjective and social dimensions of female experience are not just valued in their own right but are integrated into a larger process of delineating feminine identity. Carol Ann Howells notes that stories told by women "challenge traditional notions of gender encoded through social fictions and through narrative, unsettling the boundaries between masculine and feminine."[8] Women's narratives contest the patriarchal social order, "throwing the story-line of gender open to question and arguing for a redefinition of feminine gender identity to include many feelings and aspirations that have been rejected within traditional definitions of the feminine."[9] These texts simultaneously depict the complexities and contradictions of femininity from identifiably female centred vantage points and provide critiques of current patriarchal values, attitudes, and explanations of gender roles.

In the case of minority women, who must deal with a cultural reformulation of identity, the development of femininity can be complicated and provisional. According to Linda Hutcheon, gender "intensifies the doubleness of [sociocultural] alienation" experienced by the female ethnic subject.[10] Added to and interwoven with constructions of femininity are the social and psychological conditions that flow out of the cultural otherness of the minority female subject in Canadian society. Gender then becomes attached to ethnicity and class and, in the case of visible minority women, it also is related to the issue of race. Augie Fleras and Jean Leonard Elliott observe that although "each of these factors [gender, ethnicity, and race] remains a primary organizing principle in social relations . . . the interplay of these dimensions not only mutually reinforce the effects of the others; a hierarchy of overlapping oppressions sometimes known as multiple jeopardies is also created."[11]

In general, there appears to be a commonality of viewpoints between male and female minority writers arising from social and cultural factors specific to immigration and adjustment. This collective sense is reflected in their fiction, which to a large extent concentrates on a discourse about ethnic subjectivity. Such an observation about communality has been alluded to by Vera Golini in her essay on minority women writers and made by Caroline Morgan Di Giovanni in her analysis of the portrayal of women in minority literature.[12] However, according to Golini, female writers make use of "a female perspective to examine the images of immigrant and non-immigrant women."[13] The salience of a gendered perspective prevents the texts of male and female writers from becoming interchangeable with each other and thus part of an ideologically and culturally homogeneous representation of ethnicity. As it has been noted elsewhere, women, especially women writers, are involved in interpreting "'a woman' for themselves and for each other."[14] This act of interpretation takes place in a historically and culturally specific context: "In Canada women writers of immigrant origin have had to look into their history to create a female reality and to give voice to that reality."[15]

The presence of gender stereotyping and conventional views of femininity and masculinity are not limited to fiction that puts maleness at its centre. Such a traditional representation of gender is also evident in literary work that focuses on femininity. It is instructive to look at the fictional texts of male and female minority writers to see how these texts approach the representation of gender within the context of patriarchy in specific ethnic communities. In conducting its analysis of selected literary texts by minority writers, this essay will first examine the work of male and female Italian Canadian writers. In their fiction, these writers focus on the representation of gender from the perspective of a European based ethnicity. Also, Italian ethnicity in Canada is representative of the European immigration that took place in Canada soon after World War Two, and which has been eclipsed by the coming of immigrants to Canada, since the late 1960s and early 1970s to the present day, from developing countries. Canadians whose origins are in developing countries today are the main source of immigration to Canada. The writers of fiction from these diverse cultural and racial communities in Canada present a more immediate perspective on the process of immigration, including social and cultural adjustment, and the construction of new cultural and gender identities. As such, the fictional work of three writers of South Asian origin also will be examined: *Wife* by Bharati Mukherjee (1990), *No New Land* (1991) by M.G. Vassanji, and *Homer In Flight* by Rabindranath Maharaj (1997).[16]

At some point in the representation of gender, male Italian Canadian writers invoke ideological assumptions that they seem to be contesting. In *Black Madonna* (1982) by F. G. Paci, *Lives of the Saints* by Nino Ricci (1990), and *Drowning in Darkness* (1994) by Peter Oliva, the female protagonists are faced with a crisis of identity in a patriarchal social structure that severely constrains their ability to achieve a form of autonomy.[17] These novels also explore the contradictions of a male dominated society in which the Italian-descended male characters belong to a hierarchical class system and most often inhabit its lower rungs. Male authority and male-based norms about gender roles have been destabilized and eroded by immigration and socioeconomic displacement. While weaving this kind of critical view of reality, *Black Madonna*, *Lives of the Saints*, and *Drowning in Darkness* promote at some level in their narrations about the lives of the female protagonists a "masculinist perspective."[18]

In *Black Madonna*, Marie Barone, one of the two main characters, is insistent in her rejection of the values and habits of a patriarchal and matrifocal family structure. Preparing for an academic career that would liberate her from the shackles of domesticity, she angrily tells her mother that "There is more to the world, Ma, than cooking and keeping house for a man. You don't understand. A girl has to make a living for herself."[19] Marie's opposition to traditional womanhood is inseparable from her renunciation of her mother's cultural heritage: "You still live in the old country. You don't understand anything about this place."[20] The proponent of traditional femininity (traditional femininity entails that personal needs and aspirations are to be sacrificed for the creation of family) is Assunta, who bel-

ligerently tries to mould Marie into her own image of a
dutiful wife and mother. Interestingly enough, Marie turns
to her father for support in her struggle against her over-
bearing mother. From Marie's point of view, Adamo
appears to be understanding and sensible in comparison to
the ogre like Assunta.

Underlying the conflict between immigrant mother and
Canadianized daughter is the opposition of cultural values:
Italian femininity is perceived by Marie to be an obstacle to
social mobility in mainstream society. Marie's relinquishing
of her academic career to help her English Canadian husband, who pursues a doctorate in philosophy, and to take
care of their son epitomizes this barrier. However, the depiction of the patriarchal nature of the Canadian mainstream
demonstrates that assimilation, as a way out of the gender
inequality in the Italian community, is ultimately illusory.
Marie's life is circumscribed by patriarchy and she seems to
exchange one form of servitude for another as she moves
from Sault Ste. Marie to Toronto. This type of social commentary is linked to Marie's reconciliation with the spirit of
her dead mother: she builds a shrine to her memory and
reappropriates the traditional Italian femininity she had dis-
carded. The novel attempts to create a balance between the
private and the public realm, and between cultural retention
and the necessities of assimilation. Marie's journey to Italy to
attend her cousin's wedding signifies her attachment to the
old culture and, by association, her participation indicates
sympathy for one of the primary rituals of traditional womanhood. In this case, her cousin's marriage marks her entry
into her own household and the continuance at a more
intense and extensive level of her domestic role. Nevertheless, Marie maintains her ties to mainstream society,
although her relationship with Richard remains unresolved.

Black Madonna, however, cannot purge itself of patriarchal assumptions about gender, which it is trying to
question, and deconstruct. The "Madonna" figure carries
multifarious meanings. She symbolizes the adversity of a
Catholic peasant community in rural Italy and of working
class immigrants in the host country, the suffering of the
Italian peasant and immigrant woman as embodied by
Assunta, and the destructive and creative powers of the
feminine principle. However, the overriding emphasis on
motherhood as a primary marker of femininity invokes the
cult of the mother as a strong component of Italian patriarchy. Such a male-centred view is reinforced by the representation of the mind and body split: Marie represses
her sexuality and harnesses the power of her intellect.
While this division signifies the break between an organic
Italian culture and urban, technological Canadian society,
it denotes patriarchy's devaluation of emotion and the
privileging of the intellect, which is another way of sepa-
rating the private from the public sphere. Although in
entering traditional femininity Marie reappropriates the
physical, the intuitive, and the elemental, it is the
"Madonna" construct and its ideological allusions that are
reinvigorated at the end of the novel. Although binaries in
the text, such as mind and body, intuitive and rational, old
and new culture, preindustrial and industrial, continually
collapse into each other because of internal contradictions, they send back to the reader a discourse which
inheres from a positivist patriarchal culture. *Black
Madonna* seems to exhibit sensitivity to issues connected
to gender and ethnicity in two opposed but interconnect-
ed male dominated social environments. Yet, the novel still
maintains an affiliation with patriarchal notions of femininity which it scrutinizes and treats ironically.

The ideological recourse to patriarchy is repeated in *Lives of the Saints*. The novel's examination of the debilitating effects of a male oriented agrarian community on a woman who espouses contemporary views about femininity is subtextually at cross-purposes with its intrinsic valorization of traditional womanhood. Told from the point of view of a young boy, the narrative makes ambiguous connections between young Vittorio's sexual fantasies about his female teacher and the erotic undertones of Vittorio bathing with his mother in the caves. In the two scenes not only is the objectification of the female body at the core of the central character's awareness of femininity but the maternal figure is also the source of his awakening sexuality. The subtle blurring of mother and lover leads us back to a patriarchal idea about the place of the woman in Italian peasant society. The mythological intonations of the Cristina figure as goddess, saint, and martyr supplement the text's sombre yet adoring view of motherhood. Cristina defies the existing social order to achieve self-actualization unlike her hagiographic namesake who rejected Roman civilization in favour of a more humane and spiritual community. The differences between the two Cristinas are lessened, however, by the fact that they are ideologically intertwined through their association with the self-effacing qualities of traditional womanhood.

Another component that diminishes the credibility of the feminine perspective in the novel is the depiction of the peasant women as being callous towards Cristina, given her predicament. Their hopes for a better life than that of their mothers have been smashed by the harshness of subsistent agrarianism. Also, the striving for autonomy has been arrested by the strictures of a hierarchical male order. The women collaborate openly with the village patriarchy, ostracizing Cristina, whom many of them have known since childhood, and they attempt to force her into a state of repentance and subservience. This negative portrayal of the peasant women as backward, vicious, and conspiratorial stands in marked contrast to the aggrieved figure of the ship's captain's wife. Aboard the passenger liner as it prepares to set sail for Canada, Cristina offers her sympathy and emotional support to the woman. Ironically the captain, like Cristina, has engaged in adultery. Although all the women in the novel have been subjected to different forms of oppression in patriarchal society, they are not all necessarily presented favourably.

What the novel suggests is that the antagonism between Cristina and the other women is not just about differing views of femininity but about class positioning. Her childhood friend, Giuseppina, who is becoming increasingly estranged from Cristina, tells her, "You can't afford to walk around like a princess. It turns people against you."[21] As the daughter of the village patriarch, who had been aligned with the ruling political order, especially during the fascist regime, Cristina has had a social status unobtainable by the other women. The waning of her father's influence in the hamlet after the war appears to be consonant with the loss of his ability to control his daughter's behaviour, and, ironically, to some extent, his decline encourages Cristina's disobedience and subversion of traditional norms. However, the conflict between the women and Cristina mostly comes out of their long-standing resentment towards her privileged position in the village. Although they attack her because of her infidelity, this behaviour is in actuality part of the way they get their revenge on her for Cristina's higher social status and haughtiness. The reprisal is made possible now because of the diminution of her father's standing in Valle del Sole. Instead of showing that Cristina and the rest of the women are victims of the same forces of economic and gender oppression and therefore share a kind of solidarity in their struggles against the status quo, the text differentiates normatively between acceptable and non-acceptable women.

The novel uses the idea of "progress," which derives from technological and urban society, to set up its "feminist" criteria. Cristina supposedly is advanced in her behaviour and thinking because she has emancipatory views about women's relations to men and about sexuality. Of all the female characters, she is the only one who is worldly, as evidenced by her self-confidence in interacting with others in the city below the village, and especially when she is in the company of men. In contrast, the other women have no sense of self, are crude in their demeanour, and backward in outlook, because they are part of an oppressive past, a retrograde agrarian culture and society. Notions of modernity are linked inextricably to social class, since Cristina and the captain's wife are women whose status is superior to that of the other women. Compared to the female villagers, the two women are rendered in a noticeably sympathetic manner. The examination of gender oppression is highly problematic in the way that the novel mixes social class with ideas about progress and an autonomous femininity. The emancipatory aspect of *Lives of the Saints* appears to be put under serious doubt by a sequence of incongruities which call attention to an underlying classist and phallocentric view of what constitutes a positive female identity.

Peter Oliva's *Drowning in Darkness* resuscitates certain archetypal images of masculinity and femininity that, in their own ways, admit to the binary nature of patriarchal culture. The narrative works by opposing the masculine to the feminine. Sera, the female protagonist, is endowed with qualities that are allied with a woman's role as nurturer. In

contrast, the male characters, as exemplified by her husband, Pep, are depicted as subhuman louts who use the
force of their bodies in response to a dangerous and oner-
ous industrial environment. Sera transforms Pep from an
unkempt and coarse miner to a neat, orderly, and caring
husband. Sunderd, whom Sera seeks out in her loneliness
and despair, is unable to break out of his detachment and
cynicism despite his compassion towards her and an affinity for the natural environment. This is partly a reaction to
the futility of his work as a medical doctor in the face of
the continual carnage at the mine, and partly a result of his
feeling of disempowerment as a man in industrial society.
The men, most of whom are immigrants, are deeply alienated because of the tremendous physical hardship of mining and the severe economic exploitation of their labour by
the mining company. The mining town, depicted as barren
and severe, is equally oppressive for the women who cannot construct a solid base for family and community. The
novel does not indicate, however, that there is a sense of
solidarity among the men and the women in the struggle
against poverty, physical deprivation, and the use of cheap
labour. Instead the women abandon the men because the
ambience and operations of the mining industry are antagonistic to their feminine sensibilities: "A lot of the women
didn't like it here, couldn't stand the Pass . . . a lot of them
left one way or another."[22] The lack of class and ethnic fel-
lowship among the women and the men is partially the
result of the greediness of the men, who work long hours,
neglect their wives, and constantly put their lives at risk in
order to make as much money as they can. The estrange-
ment is also the product of an environment in which men
at all social levels seem unconcerned with building family
and community.

Woven into the rendering of the factors that shape the

social and economic conditions of the townspeople is the notion that there are certain traits inherent in men and women that predispose them to a kind of strife which becomes especially pronounced in an industrial setting. This idea leads to the gender binarism of the novel, which reveals itself in terms of "male" and "female" locales. The bleakness, the suffocating atmosphere, and the psychological and physical violence of the mining town, symbolic of a technological, and male-centred society, are contrasted to an idyllic community in Calabria, renowned for its lineage of mighty women who sustain a sea-bound village through their labour and curative abilities. This polarity, functioning as a symbolic representation of the opposition of English Canadian and Calabrian/Italian culture, serves to strengthen the notion of an essentialist maleness and femaleness.

Sera is bestowed with civilizing abilities which are deployed in fulfilling the traditional role of the wife as domesticator and as provider of emotional and sexual comfort. Because of his exposure to these feminine attributes, Pep, her husband, is divested of his brutishness and actualizes his sense of masculinity. The desolation of industrial society and Pep's failure to free himself from the prison of work and economic ambition are so overwhelming that his wife yearns to return home to a hospitable and feminine social ambience. Sera's mind is filled with memories of what she has left behind: "The past lived in her dreams. Mediterranean people from other lifetimes – ghosts from her childhood – washed in out of Sera's dreams."[23] The protagonist's dislocation in Canada (which eventually results in her desertion of her husband and a kind of spiritual death on her part, symbolized by her disappearance into the mouth of a mine shaft) is not just a consequence of having to cope with the expectations of traditional womanhood. Such womanhood immersed in mythic allusions to a village-based Calabrian femininity cannot secure a place for itself in a male dominated industrial society. It is this underlying idea that femaleness can only naturally occupy certain spaces that gives assent to the patriarchal categorization of gender roles. While the valorization of traditional femininity, characterized in terms of the healing arts, domesticity, and community building, points to the pivotal role played by women in immigrant enclaves, the opposition and reification of qualities conventionally associated with men and women undermines the "feminist" perspective in the text.

When we turn to examine the work of female Italian Canadian writers, such as *The Lion's Mouth* (1993) by Caterina Edwards, *Infertility Rites* (1991) by Mary Melfi, and *Surface Tension* by Marisa De Franceschi (1994), we begin to see that, although femininity is involved in patriarchally-based cultural processes, the trajectory of the writing is directed away from the assumptions of the prevailing social order.[24] In these novels, written more or less at the same time as the cited male texts, from the 1980s to the 1990s, there is a recurrent portrayal of the female protagonists as being primarily professional women. They have consciously fashioned a life for themselves outside the traditional structures of patriarchal femininity. The cultural and social positioning of the central characters in the public sphere is itself an indication of the ideological underpinnings of the fictional texts. The crises faced by the women in the fiction take various forms and in great part are activated by the dilemmas of living in conflicting cultural settings.

Identity formation in Edward's, Melfi's, and De Franceschi's novels, however, is not joined solely to the issue of culture, of choosing among an evolving host of values and lifestyles. It is framed in terms of gender relations, of the placement of the woman in an urban society that is mainly organized around male ideas about womanhood. The female protagonist in each of the novels has to overcome barriers that attempt to forestall her autonomy and keep her within the household. Often she internalizes the emotional, sexual, and social tendencies of patriarchal society, only to discover that the male figure is not her protector and saviour but part of a socioeconomic system which is designed to confine her. Although *The Lion's Mouth*, *Infertility Rites*, and *Surface Tension* stress, in their own manner, that a feminine self constructed out of female desire and experience remains tentative within the power arrangements of patriarchy, there is an understanding, whether implicit or explicit, that the fissure between the private and the public, the intuitive and the rational, Italian and Canadian culture, is endemic to traditional maleness.

In the three novels, aspects of womanhood (wifehood, maternity, and domesticity) are presented as social and cultural constructs. This fiction constantly overlays the intuitive with the rational, private with public space, since femininity is seen as a set of choices that a woman makes out of an array of social options and therefore a woman is not limited to customary ways of being female. Instead of mythologizing motherhood or glamourizing maternal traits, *The Lion's Mouth*, *Infertility Rites*, and *Surface Tension* focus their attention on the female protagonist's dissatisfaction with male-centric views of femininity. These texts also explore the respective protagonist's attempts to negotiate a feminine identity in a field of contradictory actions and attitudes. The framework of this negotiation is not tilted in favour of the private to the detriment of the public or vice versa.

In *The Lion's Mouth*, nurturing and creativity, normally

ascribed to womanhood, drive Bianca Bolcato's work as a writer. At the same time, the power of the intellect and the self-reliance she has achieved as an artist, as a professional woman, are utilized to humanize her social and natural environment. Throughout the narrative, there is an awareness on the part of the protagonist that her identity is not only multiple and inconsistent, but that the surrounding social and cultural contexts are involved in constant change and are highly unstable. Storytelling becomes the means through which Bianca can document this endless process of evolution and combustion and can open up new modes of seeing the world. As the protagonist-narrator admits, "With me, it is always stories. And in the end it is all I can offer you."[25] Femininity is unclosed, forever creating and recreating itself within a terrain of competing and interlocking cultural and gender beliefs and values.

The use of satire and parody in *Infertility Rites* subverts not only the privileging of public space, the pursuit of a professional career in a socioeconomic system typified by its consumerism and gender inequality. Satire and parody legitimize the desire to nurture, to have a child in reaction to the emptiness of urban, capitalist society. At the same time, satire and parody underline the shortcomings of motherhood, since motherhood is a social construct and not just a biological impulse on a woman's part. The emotional and creative are intermingled in the novel: the traumas of reproduction offer material for the paintings of Nina, the central character, and her determination to have a baby is tinged with the same obsessive drive which marks her artistic endeavours. In the end, motherhood remains hypothetical, for in and of itself, motherhood cannot solve the difficulties of feminine identity and ethnicity which are imbedded in a set of social and cultural settings that are paradoxical and alterable. The sarcastic tone and poetic

allusiveness that underlie the narrator-character's enunciation of motherhood capture the novel's unromantic view
of maternity within the limits of patriarchal society and its
affirmation of child rearing as a powerful element of feminine identity: "Oh yes to the wonderful shape of babies' little hands and feet, so clever and so inspirational. May your
generation guarantee the Dove's supremacy. Welcome."[26]

Surface Tension mobilizes many of the motifs and
strategies that are present in *The Lion's Mouth* and
Infertility Rites (such as irony, role playing, and a self-con-
scious narrator-character) to emphasize the fact that feminine minority identity is a product of multifarious social
forces and not a conglomeration of natural tendencies. The
protagonist has been able to balance her professional
career with her role as wife and mother. Margaret Croff's
dissatisfaction with her husband, who is often disconnect-
ed from his emotional life and who reproduces ideas about
masculinity which derive from patriarchal society, is itself
an expression of her disapproval of a conventional maleness that is divided according to body and mind. In Daniel,
she finds a man who is able to bring several traits together.
The convergence of the physical, the emotional, the sexual, the intellectual, and the imaginative in Daniel mirrors
her own desire for completion. Although her relationship
with her husband, who is a creature of consumer capitalist
society, is a reenactment of the inequality of power relations between men and women, Margaret's love affair with
Daniel is characterized by emotional and social reciprocity.
Her liaison with Daniel, her decision to leave her husband,
and her painful acceptance of her son's departure from
home are evidence of her endorsement of a feminine self
that is not circumscribed by patriarchal womanhood.

Surface Tension evokes an indefinite and irrational
world in which there is no solid cultural and social ground

upon which a woman's identity can be built. As the narra-tor-protagonist tells the reader, "Things change. Nothing is constant."[27] The uncertainty and injustice of human exis-tence, dramatized through the unexpected and tragic deaths of other characters in the novel who die in child-hood and in their prime, are coupled with the idea that social relations are unpredictable and unstable. Even the conclusion of the novel, as Margaret flies to Italy to be with Daniel, who is aged and ailing, is suffused in ambivalence as she ponders the possibility of a plane crash. Her union with Daniel does not seem to remove her underlying anxi-ety about the arbitrariness and impermanence of existence. Moving back and forth in a series of roles, as lover, wife, mother, friend, and professional woman, Margaret is not anchored in any of these parts that comprise her ever shift-ing identity. At the end of the novel, she is poised away from a sense of self that involves a relationship with a man, having left her husband and expecting the impending death of her terminally ill lover. Although Margaret acknowl-edges that she has been shaped by the forces of patriarchy within the Italian family and community and within English Canadian society, she resists the constraints placed on women's freedom. In her own way she develops a defi-nition of femininity that is multidimensional and that allows her to express her potential as a person and make contact with different facets of her humanity. Like the cen-tral characters in *The Lion's Mouth* and *Infertility Rites*, the female protagonist of *Surface Tension* does not idealize tra-ditional womanhood. Margaret Croff refuses to adhere to a set of givens that would delimit the scope of what con-stitutes contemporary femininity.

In the cited fiction by women of Italian origin, Caterina Edwards, Mary Melfi, and Marisa De Franceschi, the diverse representations of gender are conducted from ideological and cultural perspectives that differ markedly from those of the male writers. Particularly significant is the way in which the men go about depicting the female minority subject. This disparity in the literary portrayal of gender demonstrates that women writers are not just handling issues associated with ethnicity and identity formation in a unique fashion. Women's writing as a whole, in the context of the analysis provided in this essay, avoids being another variation on such recurrent themes as immigration, displacement, inter-generational conflict, and cultural change. Instead it provides within the overall framework of minority experience a viewpoint that contests some of the fundamental beliefs that are considered to be part of that history and social development. The fiction of minority women writers compels the reader to reassess suppositions about family, community, and identity, and therefore to rethink in a serious manner values and beliefs that have been deemed to be central to the evolution of ethnicity in the Italian Canadian community. This fiction indicates that the body of literature of a specific group of people is not culturally and ideologically homogenous. It is reflective of the kinds of conflict that underlie relations of power within the minority community and between that community and the dominant society.

The differences in the representation of gender in the above cited work of male and female Italian Canadian writers is also evident in the selected literary texts of South Asian Canadian writers. To begin with, M. G. Vassanji's *No New Land* presents a particular story about the South Asian immigrant experience in Toronto. The story is told in the third person and mainly from the perspective of Nurdin Lalani, who immigrated to Canada with his wife and young daughter during the political turmoil in eastern Africa that followed the political independence of the area's countries from Britain in the 1950s and early 1960s. The South

Asian communities in such eastern African countries as Tanganyika, Kenya, and Uganda were linked economically and politically to the European colonial apparatus. When European political control ended in the region, the various African countries, in the process of actualizing their sense of cultural nationalism, dismantled the administrative and economic structures that had been put in place by the European powers. At the same time, the leadership of these newly formed African nations began to ostracize members of the South Asian community who had collaborated with the elite of the European colonial system. It is this experience of political instability, economic loss, and cultural and social displacement which precedes the central character's immigration to Canada.

In Toronto, Nurdin Lalani is unable to reestablish the social and economic status that he had lost in east Africa. Conditioned to be the decision-maker and the sole economic provider for his wife Zera and daughter Fatima, Nurdin internalizes his sense of powerless in the new society. The traditional division of labour in his household, in which his wife does the domestic chores and the care giving and he attends to the practicalities of economic survival, is also attached to conventional ideas about masculinity and femininity. However, the text does not seem to infer that Zera is as dissatisfied as Nurdin with the downward mobility experienced by the movement to Canada. There is a social and cultural continuity to her life. What might have changed for her are the setting and the kind of people whom she needs to deal with socially. But her essential role as a woman and her personal identity have remained largely unchanged.

In contrast, Nurdin is in a state of anxiety and confusion. Much of this emotional turmoil is manifested through his sexuality. Desiring to have sex with his wife, he believes

that marriage and parenthood have now made the fulfill-
ment of such desire no longer possible. His wife has
become unattractive to him sexually and emotionally
because their relationship is based on the conventional
roles that they perform as husband and wife and as parents
to their young daughter. As the son of a successful and
wealthy businessman, and as an educated and skilled
entrepreneur, in Toronto he is forced to do demeaning
work as a counter clerk at a donut shop and as a caretaker
at the Ontario Addiction Centre. So, expressing his desire
for a woman and wanting to exercise his sexual urges
become for Nurdin the ways that he can reassert his masculine identity in the face of his experience of economic
and social disenfranchisement.

His friendship with an attractive widow named Sushila,
who had been the daughter of the cobbler in his hometown
in east Africa, slowly turns romantic. Despite the mutual
feelings of sexual and emotional attraction between
Nurdin and Sushila, their relationship is never consummat-
ed. Burdened by guilt and unable to shake off his sense of
inadequacy as a man, Nurdin remains faithful to his wife.
But his faithfulness to his wife is not predicated on passionate love or emotional intimacy. The social freedom that
is available to him in Toronto is undermined by the social
strictures of his traditional marriage to Zera, and by his
economic and social marginality as an immigrant in
Toronto. However, he is unable to totally keep his sexual
and emotional urges under control. In a highly ambiguous
scene, which takes place while he is working at the Ontario
Addiction Centre, he attempts to help a white female client
who has fallen on the floor. But the nearness of her body
and the smell of her body odour fill him for a fraction of a
second with an overwhelming sense of desire. The woman's claim that he has attempted to assault her sexually

does not technically reflect his behaviour, since he does not abuse her physically. In addition, he is eventually found to be innocent of the charge in court. Nonetheless, Nurdin Lalani seems to believe in his own mind that thinking about having sex with someone and feeling sexual desire for someone are as wrong morally and legally as actually being unfaithful or sexually abusive.

What is interesting about the description of the particular incident at the Addiction Centre and the overall representation of masculinity and femininity is the way that the novel, *No New Land*, brings together a number of complex issues. First, the book makes inferences to the complexities of cultural and social adjustment. The narrative insinuates that deviant behaviour is automatically attributed to an immigrant, especially an immigrant of colour, who crosses over certain, implied social boundaries – such as in this case making physical contact with a white woman. Also the book makes allusions to the loss of economic status that is experienced by educated and skilled immigrants, underscoring the racist nature of contemporary capitalist society. At the same time, whether Nurdin Lalani accepts it or not, the book indicates that immigration also necessitates the reformulation of ethnic identity. This reformulation, by the force of circumstance, involves social class, the intersection of South Asian/African culture and English Canadian culture, and the reworking of ideas and beliefs related to masculinity and femininity.

The sense of powerlessness that Nurdin feels at the social, emotional, and sexual levels of human experience is emblematic of the loss of the social status and cultural pride that was associated with his cultural heritage as a South Asian living in Africa. Immigration to Canada does not diminish the sense of loss he experienced in East Africa. Ironically, the country that supposedly promises political, social, and personal freedom, sustains the kind of degradation that Nurdin went through in his homeland. At the same time, the representation of femininity is intrinsically connected to the male-based perspective of the central character. The various female characters seem to be reduced to specific stock types: the sexless and domineering wife, the attractive and sensual widow who ultimately is not devoted to him, and the women in the sex trade, whose bodies are only available to him if he pays for their services. None of the main female characters in the book seem to be presented as being complex, multi-dimensional human beings. The narrator does not enter their minds, thus preventing the reader from obtaining a sense of what they feel and how they see the world around them. Instead most of the female characters appear to exist, to a great extent, as projections of the central character's troubled and unstable consciousness. Moreover, the conventional portrayal of femininity reinforces a patriarchal view of the roles of women in contemporary society.

Rabindranath Maharaj's *Homer in Flight* also depicts South Asian experience in suburban Ontario, but it does so from within the specific context of Trinidadian culture. The novel examines how immigration to Canada and the process of adjustment transform traditional notions about femininity and masculinity. Presented from the perspective of the central character, Homer Santokie, the novel exposes the contradictions that inhere from the attempt to maintain one's ethnic identity while adopting the beliefs and values of an urban, consumerist society, where everything is treated as a commodity. Determined to make a new life in Canada, Homer believes that his education and work experience from Trinidad will allow him to get a well-paying office job. The challenge will be to effectively market himself by sending out letters of applications and copies of his resumé. He aspires to a materialistic life, which is marked by the acquisition of a new car, "[n]ot one the *rackatang* matchboxes favoured in Trinidad but a roomy American model with power this and that,"[28] and the eventual purchase of a subdivision home, like the one that his cousin Grants has. To complete this vision of life in Canada, Homer thinks of meeting a young woman and getting married. Marriage and family are intrinsically part of the contemporary consumerist lifestyle. Like the other commodities that he will acquire, a wife will provide him with certain practical benefits, such as a well-kept orderly house and regular meals, and of equal importance a wife will reinforce his social status.

When he fails to get the job he wants as a clerk in an office, the kind of job that he had in a government agency in Trinidad, Homer is forced to accept work in a factory, where fruit juice and other sweetened beverages are produced. Not only does he find the work physically taxing, but he also believes it to be demeaning, to be an affront to his education and social class. Demoralized and depressed, Homer accepts a fellow worker's suggestion that he needs to be in the company of women. But to his surprise, Scrunch brings Homer to a local bar whose main form of entertainment is exotic dancing. When Homer pays for a private dance by one of the performers, he is both repulsed and sexually stimulated by the woman. Unable to contain himself any longer, Homer "found a desperate strength, tossed [the dancer] aside and ran out of the building."[29] There is an ambiguity to Homer's behaviour, not simply because he is ashamed of himself in being incapable of controlling his sexual urges in a public environment, but because he is getting sexual gratification from a situation which prevents him from fulfilling his sexual desire. Homer's behaviour is not motivated by the awareness that the objectification of women's bodies for men's pleasure is a symptom of the way that male-based society oppresses women. His decision to leave the bar comes out of his sexual frustration and overall powerlessness to assert his sense of self as a man in the new society.

In Trinidad, Homer did not have to pay to make social contact with a woman or to engage in sexual activity with her. He believed that his self confidence, his charm, and physical attractiveness drew women to him. After he quits his job at the fruit juice plant, he wanders aimlessly through the local malls, observing the various kinds of single and married women who shop there. He scrutinizes their physical appearance, and fantasizes about being with them. His behaviour at the shopping malls indicates that Homer does engage in the objectification of women, focusing on their bodies, and seeing them as objects of his sexual desire. The presence of the women at the shopping malls affirms what he considers to be one of the most important qualities of being a male: being able to attract women. For Homer Santokie, women exist only in relation to men, for their sense of femininity can only be actualized when they find certain men desirable and when these men reciprocate in kind. Furthermore, his self-worth seems connected to him sharing the company of a woman. Unemployed and socially isolated, Homer attempts to increase his self-esteem by starting a relationship with a woman.

When Homer meets a young South Asian woman from Trinidad, named Vashti, in the laundry room in his apartment building, and subsequently develops a relationship with her, it is not passion or a set of common interests that binds him to her. Instead it is emotional neediness caused by his failure to find the job he wants and his lack of social ties. He eventually marries Vashti not out of love or a shared vision of life, but because he knows that marriage is the only way that he can ensure that he can stay with her, fearful that if he loses her he will be totally lost in Canada. At the same time, he does not approve of her efforts to become a contemporary Canadian woman, who wants to improve her education and pursue a career. Homer does not really understand the reason why Vashti had refused to marry an older, well-to-do Indian man, whom her parents had chosen for her, in Trinidad. Homer thought that she had rejected the man because she was not attracted to him, and that she did not like his unromantic, business-oriented attitude towards the proposed marriage. Her parents' insistence that Vashti should enter an arranged marriage prompted her eventual immigration to Canada, where she believed she would be socially and economically independent as a woman. Vashti left Trinidad because she wanted to avoid the fate that awaited her there: she did not want to be a traditional wife, accepting a subservient position in marriage. Yet, to a large extent, this is the kind of role that Homer wants Vashti to perform in their marriage, expecting her to fulfill him, emotionally and socially.

Encoded in the narrative's exploration of Homer's consciousness is the cultural dichotomy that he has accepted as a means to meet his emotional and sexual needs and to maintain his authority over women and thus his social status as a man. Having married Vashti out of the desire for female companionship, for the benefits that derive from the nurturing abilities of femininity, Homer assumes that she will take care of him physically and emotionally as his mother had done at home in Trinidad. However, as his past sexual relationships with women in Trinidad and his sexual desire for Canadian women at the shopping malls indicate, that nurturing femininity is separated from an eroticized femininity. The woman whom Homer wants to be involved with sexually exists primarily on the basis of her eroticism and is attractive to him precisely because she is not a nurturer.

In the novel, the use of irony and satire commingle constantly to draw out the subtleties and complexities of Homer's feelings and attitudes. These two literary devices also are used to demonstrate that all levels of social life and all forms of cultural identifications are socially constructed, thus they are arbitrary and highly unstable. The employment of satire and irony allow the reader to glean the many contradictions imbedded in the personality of the given character, especially that of Homer, making connections in the process between personality and social structure. However, Homer himself never gains true insights into the nature of the social structures he is part of, and remains mostly unaware of the inconsistencies in his behaviour and value system. Unlike Homer Santokie who constantly derides other individuals for been hypocritical, intellectually shallow, and ethically reprehensible, the reader is constantly aware that each of the characters is imperfect, contradictory, self-absorbed, and morally flexible. In this context, in deconstructing the nature of Homer's personality and his male identity through the use of irony and satire, the novel points to the ideological implications of Homer's uncritical absorption of patriarchal ideas about femininity.

Homer seems incapable of mustering the willpower to get any job that he can find. Nevertheless, even when it is only Vashti who is working to pay for their living expenses and for the rental of the basement suite in her sister's suburban home, Homer still expects her to attend to his needs. He is also unhappy that Vashti spends so much time socializing with her sister and her friends. He is threatened by the increasing influence that his sister-in-law, Jay, has over Vashti, an influence that is mostly the result of his inability to communicate with his wife. When Homer eventually finds a job as a librarian in a local elementary school, he demands that Vashti, who is pregnant at time, move out of Jay's house with him and that the two of them rent an apartment. Her refusal to leave with Homer is not just the result of the lack of communication, his inability to express his feelings, and his insensitivity to her emotional needs. She decides to stay with her sister during her pregnancy because Homer showed very little interest in her when she told him she was pregnant.

Homer's subsequent separation from Vashti accelerates the disintegration of their marriage. Homer is absent during the birth of his son, and does not begin to interact with him until he has begun to walk. At the end of the novel, Vashti is able to integrate her South Asian identity, based on familial values, exemplified by her strong bond with her sister and her love for her son, with her modern ideas of womanhood, manifested in the pursuit of a university degree and her ambition to have a successful career, as well as her relationship with her English Canadian boyfriend, which is based on equality and reciprocity. While Homer refashions his cultural identity in Canada, adopting a realistic view of what is possible to achieve in urban, capitalist society, his Canadianization does not lead to a rethinking of his sense of maleness. For his part, Homer learns to accept the existential nature of the immigrant experience. At some level this acceptance is emblematic of the social and cultural displacement that is so much the result of the entrenchment of global capitalism. It appears to be a defensive strategy against a malevolent cosmos, not an invocation of the qualities that are intrinsic to a humanistic view of the world. This darkly romantic vision of modern life reiterates Homer's masculine sense of human society. Modern society is spiritually empty, and individuals, especially men, are in a constant competition with each other, and one faced with unremitting menace and chaos. Conjuring up words that express his disillusionment with both Trinidad and Canada, words which evoke the idea that there is no ideal place to live in, that there is ultimately no promised land, Homer presents his personal philosophy about life: "'Drawing strength from our solitariness. Hermits in a hostile world. Secure in the armour of our Other Selves. Inviolate.'"[30]

In the novel *Wife*, Bharati Mukherjee deconstructs the ideological premise of traditional Indian femininity, a femininity that is defined in mostly masculine terms. Her scathing critique, in which the central character's anger and bitterness towards a patriarchal social structure are keenly invoked, is part of the process of opening up a new emancipatory space for South Asian femininity within the context of an individualistic, urban North American society, in this case the U.S.A. It should be noted that Bharati Mukherjee, who originally immigrated to Canada, and who subsequently moved to the U.S.A. with her writer husband Clark Blaise, has written fiction which depicts the experience of South Asian women in both Canada and the U.S.A.

Wife is divided into three major narrative units. The first part of the novel, which takes place in India, focuses on the central character Dimple's preoccupation with getting married and the beginning of her marriage to Amit Basu, an engineer. The second part of the book deals with Dimple and Amit Basu's immigration to the U.S.A., motivated by his desire for economic improvement, and the process of social and cultural adjustment. The third part of the book portrays the profound psychological deterioration of Dimple, as she is unable to find any purpose and meaning in her role as a wife, and the eventual, violent end of her relationship with Amit.

Throughout the story, the omniscient narrator describes the shifting views of Dimple Basu towards marriage and being a wife, which are embodiments of male-based ideas about the role of the woman in Indian culture. In her early twenties, Dimple enters naïvely into a traditional marriage, believing that such a marriage will fulfill her emotionally and allow her to obtain her social independence. Desperately anxious to get married, because she is worried that if she does not act quickly she will permanently lose her opportunity to become a wife, Dimple decides not to continue her studies at university. Dimple turns her back on a future in which she could pursue a professional career and become economically, if not socially, independent from a man and her immediate family. Like the heroines in romantic Indian movies, Dimple believes that marriage will provide romance and adventure and a sense of self-fulfillment as a woman. Instead, soon after her marriage, when she enters her husband's household, she is constantly judged by her mother-in-law to be inadequate as a wife, as a servant to her husband and in his household. She realizes she is caught in a loveless marriage with Amit, who does not acknowledge her emotional and social needs. Her disillusionment and emotional depression over the state of her marriage are shown in a scene when she believes she is pregnant. Filled with dread over her prospective motherhood, Dimple thinks of ways of aborting the fetus in her womb: "she could arrange to slip in the bathroom or fall down the staircase or sit on a knitting needle, though that would be too obvious to conceal."[31]

When Amit and Dimple immigrate to New York City, she hopes that she will be freed finally from the constraints in her traditional Indian marriage. Her dream of a new and independent life in America, however, does not materialize. She discovers that what has changed is the cultural environment but not her essentially subordinate position in her marriage to Amit, who is enthralled by the professional opportunities which are available to him as an engineer. Dimple begins to live a schizophrenic life. Ideas and images about North American femininity based on the emancipation of the self, both emotionally and socially, do not match the numbing routine and dreariness of her situation as a wife. Dimple is confined to her apartment and engaged in domestic activities which only benefit her husband.

Eventually Dimple becomes emotionally overwhelmed by the contradictions and gaps in her life in New York City. She finds it impossible to develop a stable sense of self in a world of conflicting social realities, namely the social and economic independence of modern American women, the dissatisfaction expressed by Americanized South Asian women, regardless of whether they are married or not, and the general passivity of the married South Asian women she encounters. The instabilities and discontinuities of relationships in mainstream American society intensify her confusion. Her friendships with supposedly emancipated South Asian women – like Ina Mullick who has an arrangement with her rich husband that allows her sexual and social freedom – are tenuous and unable to resolve her emotional crisis. The ultimate shallowness of her romantic affair with Milt Glasser, an American man, pushes her closer to the edge psychologically. Glasser is sensitive and charming, but intellectually and culturally pretentious. He seems to be interested only sexually in Dimple, as evidenced in the scene when he reads the newspaper immediately after making love to her: "She wanted to jolt him, accidentally, of course, so that he could witness her agony. He had no right to read the paper and spoil beautiful endings."[32]

By the end of the novel, it is obvious to the reader that the narrative has depicted the slow, inexorable mental unraveling of a woman whose emotional life and self-identity are thoroughly eviscerated by patriarchy. Male-based culture seems to transcend national boundaries. Traditional South Asian maleness is interchangeable with conventional North American masculinity. The illusions about femininity transmitted in popular Indian movies, in which beautiful, independent-minded, and passionate women experience a sense of personal and social liberation with heroic male lovers, are reinforced by the lack of social reality in American television soap operas which promulgate images of attractive, strong-willed and emotionally expressive women who are with men out of choice. Dimple Basu is unable to discern the difference between fact and fiction, and is unaware that most countries in the world, in this case India and the U.S.A., are fundamentally patriarchal socially and economically. Instead, she believes that her husband is solely responsible for her uneventful and non-emotional marriage, which is a pale imitation of the mass media representations of modern relationships. She does not see that he is as much a prisoner as she is to a capitalist, male social order that requires him to act according to its underlying assumptions. In the U.S.A., the clash of cultural values, in which loyalty to family and cultural group are opposed to self development in an individualistic social environment, and the lingering repression of the self that took place in India combine to produce a violent form of insanity in Dimple Basu. Her inexplicably uncontrollable but conscious physical attack on her husband, during which she stabs him repeatedly with a deadly sharp kitchen knife, is the ultimate depiction of the severity of her mental illness.

Yet the conclusion of the novel does not seem to suggest that only through violence against men can women liberate themselves from the oppression of patriarchy. Dimple's madness appears to result from her sense of

almost total impotence in having the marriage she wants
and the kind of life that such a marriage would give her.
However, her lack of consciousness about the patriarchal
nature of contemporary Indian and American society, an
absence of social awareness that stems from her emotionally motivated embracing of an imaginary femininity, presents her as being partially responsible for the failure of
her marriage. Ironically, while the U.S.A. exposes her to
illusory images of womanhood, it also provides her with
the opportunity to re-negotiate her position in her marriage to Amit, despite his attempt to stop her from going
back to school and pursuing a career. Still suffering from
a delusional psychological state, Dimple Basu believes that
like the "[w]omen on [American] television [who] got
away with murder" she can easily dispose of her husband
and find a new American lover.[33] The novel *Wife* then
depicts the harsh emotional consequences visited on the
female central character in a male-based culture, refusing
to make note of any redemptive quality in the traditional
role of wife which has been imposed on South Asian
women. But the book also implies that Dimple and Amit
Basu are selectively making use of certain aspects of traditional femininity and masculinity to maintain their Indian
cultural identities while trying to benefit from the opportunities open to them as members of a largely individual-
ist North American society.

NOTES

1. Diana Fuss, *Essentially Speaking: Feminism, Nature, and Difference* (New York: Routledge, 1989), p. 36.

2. Toril Moi, *Sexual/Textual Politics: Feminist Literary Theory* (London: Methuen, 1986), .p. 171.

3. Terry Eagleton, *Literary Theory: An Introduction* (Oxford: Basil Blackwell, 1985, p. 14.

4. *Ibid.*, p. 15.

5. *Ibid.*

6. *Ibid.*, p. 190.

7. Carol Ann Howells, *Private and Fictional Words: Canadian Women Novelists of the 1970s and 1980s* (London: Methuen, 1987), p. 32.

8. *Ibid.*, p. 184.

9. *Ibid.*, p. 186.

10. Linda Hutcheon, *Splitting Images: Contemporary Canadian Ironies* (Toronto: Oxford University Press, 1991), p. 64.

11. Fleras, Augie, and Elliott, Jean Leonard, *Unequal Relations: An Introduction to Race, Ethnic and Aboriginal Dynamics in Canada* (Toronto: Prentice Hall, 1996), p. 149.

12. Vera Golini, "Canadian Women Writers of Italian Origin," *Italian Canadiana* (Vol. 11, 1995), and Caroline Morgan Di Giovanni, "The Images of Women in Italian Canadian Writing," *ibid.*

13. Golini, *op. cit.*, p. 143.

14. Susanna Egan, "The Book of Jessica: The Healing Circle of a Woman's Autobiography," *Canadian Literature* (Spring, 1995), p. 11.

15. Joseph Pivato, *Echo: Essays on Other Literature* (Toronto: Guernica Editions, 1994), p. 152.

16. M. G. Vassanji, *No New Land* (Toronto: McClelland & Stewart, 1991); Rabindranath Maharaj, *Homer In Flight*, (Fredericton: Goose Lane, 1997); Bharati Mukherjee, *Wife* (Toronto: Penguin, 1990).

17. F. G. Paci, *Black Madonna*. (Ottawa: Oberon Press, 1982); Nino Ricci, *Lives of the Saints* (Dunvegan, Ontario: Cormorant Books, 1990); Peter Oliva, *Drowning in Darkness* (Dunvegan, Ontario: Cormorant Books, 1994).

18. Jinqi Ling, "Reading for Historical Specificities: Gender Negotiations in Louis Chu's *Eat a Bowl of Tea*." *Melus*, Vol. 20, No. 1 (Spring 1995), p. 35.

19. Paci, *op. cit.*, p. 73.
20. *Ibid.*
21. Ricci, *op. cit.*, p. 56
22. Oliva, *op. cit.*, p. 161.
23. *Ibid.*, p. 45.
24. Caterina Edwards, *The Lion's Mouth* (Toronto: Guernica Editions, 1993), originally published by NeWest Publications in 1982; Mary Melfi, *Infertility Rites* (Montreal: Guernica Editions, 1991); Marisa De Franceschi, *Surface Tension* (Toronto: Guernica Editions, 1994).
25. Edwards, *op. cit.*, p. 271.
26. Melfi, *op. cit.*, p. 182.
27. De Franceschi, *op. cit.*, p. 323.
28. Maharaj, *op. cit.*, p. 14.
29. *Ibid.*, p. 103.
30. *Ibid.*, p. 323.
31. Mukherjee, *op. cit.*, p. 31.
32. *Ibid.*, p. 198.
33. *Ibid.*, p. 213.

PUBLIC MEMORY, PRIVATE GRIEF

Reinventing the Nation's (Self)Image
Through Joy Kogawa's OBASAN

EVA C. KARPINSKI

From the moment of its publication in 1981, Joy Kogawa's
Obasan has enjoyed a status unprecedented for a book,
with the exception, perhaps, of Harriet Beecher Stowe's
Uncle Tom's Cabin – another landmark text celebrated for
its reality transforming power. Kogawa's novel has played
a mediating role in the (re)construction of the national
memory of traumatic events related to the treatment of
Japanese Canadians during World War II and has been
instrumental in the success of the redress movement.
Among other things, *Obasan* has been credited with changing a Canadian literary canon, facilitating a practice of multicultural pedagogy, and bridging the gap between writing
and political activism. It would not be an exaggeration then
to claim that by examining the influence of *one* book on
the ways Canadians have been reinventing themselves in
the classroom and in literary criticism during the last twen-
ty years, the present paper participates in a discursive production of the book as a "national heroine."

The phenomenon of *Obasan* has consequences far
beyond pedagogy and literature and can be seen as symp-
tomatic of larger shifts that race, gender, sexuality, and
other markers of difference have recently brought about in

Canadian constructions of national identity. Although it was one in a series of writing on a similar subject published in the 1970s and the early 1980s,[1] Kogawa's text has become what Christl Verduyn calls a "catalyst" for the return of the repressed content of Canadian experience and Canadian literary history as well as for the subsequent revisions of this experience, prompted by the need to acknowledge its legacy of racism and ethnocentrism.[2] In the context of women's studies, the book has facilitated the introduction of the race perspective into courses organized around gender. What follows constitutes a discussion of how this particular gendered text could cause several disruptions of the nation's (self-) image. I focus on the cultural and political work performed by *Obasan* in the context of its reception and reading. In what ways does the dominant culture benefit from its engagement with "minority" literatures like *Obasan*? Why has this particular text been embraced by the mainstream? How does it resist potential appropriations by the liberal state and remains, like a true heroine, an embattled contestatory site of different narratives of the nation's history? What subversions of nationalist discourse have been provoked by *Obasan* under the sign of the Other/Woman? To acknowledge such a tremendous impact of the cultural politics produced by and around *Obasan* means to recognize that the nation-building project is erected on the bodies of racialized and gendered "others."

The fact that the book has enjoyed such unprecedented popularity and success, has received numerous awards, has been read in academic institutions and added to multicultural school curricula, qualifies *Obasan* for what David Palumbo-Liu calls "model minority discourse," defined as "an ideological construct not coextensive with the texts themselves, but rather designating a mode of apprehending, decoding, recoding, and producing Asian American narratives."[3] As the product of a particular mode of reading and subject construction, model minority discourse suggests "resolutions to a generalized 'problem' of racial, ethnic, and gendered identities."[4] Such texts participate in the rhetoric of depoliticized self-healing that suppresses material differences and sees change as the function of individual adjustments required of ethnic subjects. To other immigrants, model minority discourse represents patterns of assimilation that other groups ought to imitate; to the dominant group, it offers a sign of possible recovery from racism, of leaving such issues behind. According to Palumbo-Liu, Asian American literature has been exploited as model minority discourse in order to affirm dominant ideologies of the self and of success, popularizing the liberal notion that racial minorities can only blame themselves for their alienation in America.[5] The issues of racism, sexism, and class differences are addressed in model minority discourse in ways acceptable to a liberal audience, through thematizing "the ethnic split," "a crisis of identity," and "healing." After all, the dominant function of model minority discourse is pedagogical. It reproduces specific minority subject positions within the hegemonic order, reinforcing the dominant culture's normative expectations of conformity and a larger ideology of individualism. In this sense, Palumbo-Liu views model minority discourse as "an exemplary case of the predisposition to read . . . according to particular psychosocial needs."[6]

There are examples of "normalizing" readings of *Obasan* that use the novel as model minority discourse, or what Roy Miki calls "resolutionary" as opposed to "revolutionary" interpretations:

all [academics] tend to incorporate a resolutionary (not revolutionary) aesthetics in their overall critical framing of the novel. The agreement seems to be that Naomi resolves her silenced past, and so establishes peace with the human rights violations that caused such havoc and grief to her, to her family, and to her community.[7]

Although some readings force the novel into this model, *Obasan* resists the rhetoric of healing and the role of model minority discourse.[8] Through its figuration of the gaping wound of racism as rape, Kogawa's text shows the interrelatedness of personal trauma and institutional violence to the collective subject. Also, it offers the possibility of "progressive redefinitions of ethnicity, class, race, and gender" as affecting political change.[9] In *Obasan*, the political is not sublimated into the personal; on the contrary, the political is foregrounded through Aunt Emily's diary, and through the appendix, showing that the personal is embedded in the political. Similarly, the role the novel played in gaining support for the redress movement – a collective and political act – gives it a political life of its own.

There is one troubling aspect in Palumbo-Liu's conception of model minority discourse. This conception renders minority literature passive by focusing on one-way flow between minority literature and majority literature and culture, namely on what the mainstream gets out of this relationship. Walter Ong's model provides a useful corrective to this pattern in that he views the relationship between minority literature and majority culture as interactive: "A minority literature often negotiates for its own identity with the majority culture and constantly redefines itself, ultimately bringing the majority culture to redefine itself, too."[10] We must be careful not to strip the authors of minoritized literature of agency in their own reading communities. So-called "minority" literature matters not only because of what it does for majority culture, but also because it deals with issues of subjectivity and identity relevant to diasporic subjects.

Typically, however, model minority discourse is praised for its lack of self-pity, bitterness, or solemnity. The case of *Obasan*'s reception confirms the mainstream's investment in the containment of minority discourse. Despite, or perhaps because of its astounding artistry and poignancy, the novel has been quickly tokenized, inviting extremely sophisticated academic analyses couched in postmodern, psychoanalytic, postcolonial, and feminist rhetoric. At the same time, Kogawa's text yields itself easily to the crude didacticism of a high school classroom, guided toward the liberal-humanist discovery that we are all human after all, that racism is bad, and that all we need to do in order to become a healthy society is to "recover" our individual and communal past. The book of such haunting poetic beauty and philosophical depth, challenging the concepts of transparent language and transparent history, is repeatedly invoked in Canadian classrooms as a cliché of "multicultural" literature. It is, after all, consistent with the fate of national heroines to be assimilable into the repertoire of national clichés.

What qualifies Kogawa's novel for the role of such a celebrated catalyst of change is its perception by the establishment as "non-threatening." This perception derives from the novel's much admired modernist qualities such as "verbal restraint," its silences, gaps, and indirections, the "poetic" language that attenuates the "mimetic" truth of the experience it describes, as well as other elliptical devices such as "juvenile perspective, fragmented memories and reveries, Western fairy tales and Japanese fables."[11]

Not without significance is also the fact that the book has been praised for its lack of "explicit political or didactic intent"[12] and that the history presented in *Obasan* receives a political/textual closure, through the actual redress and the sequel *Itsuka*. Moreover, the text, which culminates in the cataclysmic event of the (American made) nuclear explosion in Nagasaki, provides a counterbalance to Canada's responsibility for the atrocities committed against Japanese Canadians.

Attempts to turn *Obasan* into model minority discourse confirm the thesis advanced by Peggy Phelan that the production of statements about the past is always "contingent upon the material, moral, political, and psychic needs of the present – as they are understood by those in power."[13] The cultural politics around Kogawa's book, and especially the novel's quick assimilation into the mainstream of literary criticism and pedagogy, involve mechanisms of co-optation that can tame and contain even the most "disagreeable" message, revealing that the invention of national history, including the one structured around the nation's guilt, is ultimately a conserving and conservative enterprise.

However, we cannot ignore the fact that the text, to some degree, cooperates with discourses of appropriation and containment. I would argue that *Obasan* deliberately presents itself as "nonthreatening." Asian American critic Traise Yamamoto discusses this feature of Nisei women's autobiography as a masking strategy, thereby restoring agency to the writing subject. The didactic purpose of Kogawa's book accounts for its reliance on writing strategies perceived as "nonthreatening." This didactic end necessitates "the avoidance of overt conflict with those readers whom [the author] desire[s] to educate."[14] Constantly facing the risk of provoking a potentially defensive and hostile reaction among white Canadian readers, the text attempts to teach white Canada the very principles of democracy that the dominant culture espouses as its own. Selective and guarded in voicing its criticism, the narrative employs a masking device of "shaming" white Canada into a recognition of the betrayal of its own democratic standards. In fact, in *Obasan*, such overt criticism is confined to Aunt Emily's diaries, marking her position vis-à-vis history as "extreme" compared to other Japanese Canadian women. As Yamamoto writes,

> Nisei women who assume autobiographical authority must be careful to present their stories in "acceptable" terms . . . there is reluctance to speak about their experience of the camps and their feelings, a guardedness about the act of revelation.[15]

Already marginalized by their race and gender when they speak, these women employ the trope of masking which often involves tonal masking such as a matter-of-fact, ungrudging, or reasonable tone and the use of euphemisms such as "prejudice" instead of racism. Similarly, Kogawa's choice of the novel form rather than autobiography can be construed as a mask that allows for articulation of a self that is critical of Canada. Her use of narrative masking can be seen as a way of negotiating "the tension between the communal act of witnessing and the specific experiences of the individual self."[16]

So why do most critics fail to see beyond the book's masking strategies? Taking up the thesis recently put forth by Smaro Kamboureli, that "repression, psychological and political, is at the heart of the story this novel tells,"[17] on the level of individual, family, and community experience, I want to suggest that this "repression" is enacted through various readings of the novel, on the level of reception as well. The meaning of the text "depends on who reads it, as well as the conditions under which it is read."[18] Critical responses to the novel, especially those of a "humanistic" kind, seek closure to the developmental narrative of the novel's movement from silence to speech. This need for closure, healing, coming to terms with the past, is motivated by the refusal or impossibility to conceive of the nation's history as founded on racist premises. According to Marita Sturken, discourses of healing "can often be employed as forms of forgetting and depoliticization,"[19] for example, as smoothing over the disruptions of the war narratives or romanticizing them. Hence there is a tendency among the readers of *Obasan* to see in the text a resolution of the racist "episode" from the nation's past rather than an indictment of an ongoing problem of racism. One of the strategies employed by the critics is to privilege the event of internment, ignoring the presence of racism as a trauma pervading the whole text, including Naomi's pre- and post-war experiences. It is also significant that the internment finds a kind of desired historical closure in the government's apology and redress, the fact that may largely account for the novel's "safe" positioning in the national imaginary. In a way, it is the "racial unease" that prompts the critics to contain the problem of racism to a singular historical event of Pearl Harbor, while completely forgetting the pre-war hysteria of the "treacherous yellow peril." Another strategy is to identify with Aunt Emily's faith in Canada as a democratic state. After all, what better proof of Canada's liberalism do we need to invoke than the fact of *Obasan*'s actual publication for mainstream consumption? Quite predictably, Emily's liberalism invites "liberal" interpretations of the novel. However, as Smaro Kamboureli observes, because Emily never recognizes racialization as "embedded in the foundations of the Canadian state, she unwittingly reproduces the liberal ideology that justifies racism within a democratic framework."[20] It is the same mechanism that allows some white Canadians or other mainstream-oriented readers to turn *Obasan* into an optimistic token of the present "multicultural" reality by replacing "race" with "culture" in the name of Canadian benevolent plurality.

Potential readers assume subject positions of Emily (transparent readings of history) or Naomi (crisis of representation; repression). Emily focuses on "the juridico-discursive" apparatus of discrimination rather than on the genealogy of racialization operating in the socio-political discourses of power, whereas Naomi focuses on how racialization affects particular subjectivities, that is, on the subjective dimension of racism/rape. However, one argument to avoid generalization of Naomi's first person narrative as neurosis or repression is the fact that she relates not only her own story but also her community's history. According to Kamboureli, Naomi's "hysteria" has to be decoded as "a double gesture of giving away and withholding."[21] This view is consistent with my reading of the text's masking strategies. Like Naomi, Kogawa's book doesn't align itself with either of the two sides in the binary constructions of speech and silence, inside and outside, ambiguity and truth, or passivity and action. Embracing and interrogating both sides of these constructed binaries, the narrative refuses to be forced into any ideological regime that might inform the novel's critical readings.

Nevertheless, contradictory meanings can be inscribed onto the body of this text partly because it offers itself as a screen, as the body of a woman, a nonthreatening Oriental other. Undoubtedly, racialized gender politics also plays a role in the novel's reception as a paradigmatic national text of ethnic healing. Reading against this script, however, I want to acknowledge the novel's subversive use of the power of imaginative constructions of the nation through the Other/Woman. The national trauma at the heart of the story – the human rights violations against Japanese Canadians – is revealed from a gendered perspective split onto three Nikkei women: Naomi, Aunt Emily, and Obasan. Collectively, they embody a raced and gendered position of difference that leads to contesting a national identity founded upon the principles of racial and ethnic homogeneity. In the situation of war, such principles override human empathy or gender solidarity, as noted by Aunt Emily, who finds it "illogical that women, who are the bearers and nurturers of the human race, should go all out for ill will like this."[22] The contrast between the reality of forced evacuation and Aunt Emily's unwavering "humanist" faith in democracy as capable of transcending racism reveals race as precisely the trauma of Canada's national history. Racism and sexual abuse are the book's "dirty" secrets. They are linked through the figure of Naomi as survivor. They are also both linked to "rape" through the power of the racializing gaze whose manifestation ranges from the tenuously offensive stares of white Canadians to the most sinister invasion of Naomi's body by Old Man Gower.

As Marita Sturken observes, official history has an ambivalent attitude to the body of the survivor as survivors "often disrupt the closure of a particular history."[23] Trauma survivors testify through their very presence to the body's importance to memory, to the materiality of memory. Embodying personal memory, survivors participate in the processes of inscribing, producing, and giving meaning to cultural memory understood as "a field of cultural negotiation through which different stories vie for a place in history."[24] Thus survivors stand at the intersection of memory and history, where different narratives are legit-

imized so as to produce concepts of the nation and Canadianness, especially in the event of great public traumas.
Kogawa's book acts as a substitute for the survivor's body
in that it embodies and generates memories of pain that
has shattered individual, communal, and national histories. To paraphrase Cathy Caruth's words, the traumatized
text "carries an impossible history within [itself]," becoming itself "the symptom of a history that [it] cannot entirely possess."[25]

Positing the Other/Woman as an (im)possible national
subject, *Obasan* brings Canadians to the limits of understanding themselves as a nation; in fact, through this gesture, the book stages a crisis of nationalist discourses as
such, as an offshoot of the patriarchal state's attempt to
ensure the "purity" of its progeny. How can a Japanese
Canadian (or, in a different context, an African Canadian)
woman figure in the Canadian symbolic as "mother of the
nation"? At best, she can only be read as a symptom of
Canada's national guilt, deprived again of subjecthood and
citizenship rights so dear to Aunt Emily. The internment of
Japanese Canadians, which was the result of the unilateral
narrowing down of the meaning of Canadianness in the
government's vigilante action, foregrounds with a particular force the question: "Who is a Canadian?" The Japanese
Canadian subject emerges at a site of contradiction
between legal citizenship and multiple identities and identifications – cultural, racial, or religious – that the subject
inhabits and that have been voluntarily chosen and/or
imposed from without. Kogawa's *Obasan* rehistoricizes
and creates a counterdiscourse to the narratives of Canada
as an inclusive nation. Deploying the effects of discourses
of race and gender on discourses on nationalism, *Obasan*
shows that juridical citizenship signifies little in the face of
a Canadian national imaginary unable to conceive of the

Asian subject as Canadian. Race as "a powerful and negative signifier," together with gender, class, and other signifiers of difference, pushes against "the universalities of the modern state" such as citizenship, property rights, democracy, and nationalism.[26] While hoping to forestall the reenactment of the state's violence, the novel also reminds us that the state and the nation, to use David Palumbo-Liu's words, "should not be read as a monolithic (that is, not contradiction-free) entity against which the 'ethnic' [or racial subject] is simply posed,"[27] but rather that "America" [and by extension Canada] "is always in process itself."[28]

In conclusion, I want to suggest yet another way of approaching *Obasan*, namely its possible reading from the perspective of trauma research. Application of contemporary theories of trauma is promising inasmuch as *Obasan* seems to resist attempts to read it in terms of earlier psychoanalytic theories of hysteria and repression, like the one recently offered by Smaro Kamboureli. Such readings approach the complex textuality of the novel as a series of "symptoms" whose hidden "truth" has to be uncovered in the end. Besides, such a "Eurocentric" approach seems to diminish the agency of the writing subject and fails to account for the novel's "masking" strategies which have been recognized as culture-specific by Asian American critics like Yamamoto. Rather than pathologizing Naomi's reaction to the multiple traumas experienced by her in her embodiment as a gendered, racialized, historicized subject, there seems to be more promise in viewing the book from the perspective of recent psychoanalytic theories of trauma. Trauma research has helped us learn more about the traumatic reaction to violent events, in both individual and group survivors. It challenges us to a new task, namely that of learning to listen to trauma beyond its pathology and to understand its human effects.[29]

Following Freud's late insight into the relation between trauma and history, Caruth writes that the structure of trauma consists

> not in the forgetting of a reality that can hence never be fully known, but in an inherent latency within the experience itself. The historical power of the trauma is not just that the experience is repeated after its forgetting, but that it is only in and through its inherent forgetting that it is first experienced at all.[30]

The inherent latency means that "the traumatic event is not experienced as it occurs, [but] it is fully evident only in connection with another place, and in another time."[31] The psychoanalytic view of the relation between crisis and survival illuminates the reaction of the Japanese Canadian community: "for those who undergo trauma, it is not only the moment of the event, but of the passing out of it that is traumatic; *survival itself*, in other words, *can be a crisis*."[32] Thus Naomi can be seen as "a witness who speaks, enigmatically, out of the crisis of [her] own survival."[33]

The critical reception of *Obasan* illustrates the difficulty of listening to and recognizing the truth of traumatic stories. The readings that reduce Naomi's adult trauma to the events of childhood, locating the origins of her traumatic experience of sexuality and race in her abuse by Old Man Gower and in the internment of Japanese Canadians, miss what Caruth identifies as the central Freudian insight into trauma, that the impact of the traumatic event lies precisely in its belatedness, in its refusal to be simply located, in its insistent appearance outside the boundaries of any single place or time.[34]

The "truth" of Naomi's trauma is situated at the intersection of personal memory, cultural memory, and official history – a site where contradictory meanings are produced and validated. Smaro Kamboureli's discussion of the continuity of racism, together with her analysis of the pre-internment racial trauma that Naomi experiences as the violence of the racializing gaze, directs our attention to the history of Japanese Canadians in Canada as a continuous struggle against racism rather than offering a consoling fiction of a single historical occurrence, a one-time error that has to be acknowledged. Kamboureli's interpretation of the novel's ending as disappointing, however, suggests the presence of tacit expectations of a "cure" or a political rather than merely aesthetic resolution. I would add that for Naomi as trauma survivor the reality of violence is still present, and the trauma of racism continues to affect her in the "present" as we see Naomi in the classroom, taunted by Sigmund (!), a white student.

Traumatic events force us to recognize the political nature of memory, individual and collective. However, trauma must be understood not only as

> a repeated suffering of the event, but also [as] a continual leaving of its site. The traumatic reexperiencing carries with it the impossibility of knowing what first constituted it. To listen to the crisis of a trauma is not only to listen for the event, but to hear in the testimony the survivor's departure from it. [35]

If in reading Naomi's story we are challenged to listen to her departure from it, our witnessing opens up the possibility of passing out of the isolation imposed by the event as well as the discourse of putting behind and forgiveness. Interestingly, Kamboureli downplays the presence of this discourse at the end of the novel, dismissing the allegorical references to Love and Grief as part of Kogawa's troubling preoccupation with religious imagery. According to Cathy Caruth, the promise of trauma studies lies in the belief that trauma itself may provide a link between cultures that goes beyond "a simple understanding of the pasts of others" – in

Obasan, the history of Japanese Canadians – the link that, "within the traumas of contemporary history [restores] our ability to listen through the departures we have all taken from ourselves."[36] Through its contestation of definitions of the nation and Canadianness, cultural memory of trauma reenacted in Kogawa's book reveals the demand for a less monolithic, more inclusive image of the nation.

NOTES

A shorter version of this paper was presented at a special session on "The Cultural Politics of *Obasan*" at the Annual Meeting of the Association of Canadian College and University Teachers Association in Edmonton, AB (May, 2000).

1. One can mention here such titles as: Shizuje Takashima's *A Child in Prison Camp* (1971); Ken Adachi's *The Enemy that Never Was* (1976); Barry Broadfoot's *Years off Sorrow, Years of Shame: The Story of the Japanese Canadians in World War II* (1977); Ann Gomer Sunahara's *The Politics of Racism: The Uprooting of Japanese Canadians during the Second World War* (1981); Takeo Ujo Nakano's *Within the Barbed Wire Fence: A Japanese Man's Account of His Internment in Canada* (1983); and Muriel Kitagawa's *Letters to Wes and Other Writings on Japanese Canadians, 1941-1948* (1985).

2. See Christl Verduyn, "Reconstructing Canadian Literature: The Role of Race and Gender" in Veronica Strong-Boag, Sherill Grace and Avigail Grace, eds., *Painting the Maple: Essays on Race, Gender and the Construction of Canada* (Vancouver: University of British Columbia Press, 1998).

3. David Palumbo-Liu, *Asian/American: Historical Crossings of a Racial Frontier* (Stanford: Stanford University Press, 1999), p. 396.

4. *Ibid.*, p. 395.

5. *Ibid.*, p. 400.

6. *Ibid.*, p. 409.

7. Roy Miki, "Asiancy: Making Space for Asian Canadian Writing," in Gary Okihiro et al., eds., *Privileging Positions: The Sites of Asian American Studies* (Pullman: Washington State University Press, 1995), p. 143.

8. I have been using the term "minority literature" following Ong and Palumbo-Liu; however, I personally prefer to use the term "minoritized literature" as indicative of the unequal power dynamics rather than ontological status of this kind of writing.

9. Palumbo-Liu, *op. cit.*, p. 399.

10. After Traise Yamada, *Making Selves, Making Subjects: Japanese American Women, Identity and the Body* (Berkeley: University of California Press, 1999), p. 306.

11. King-Kok Cheung, *Articulate Silences: Hisaye Yamamoto, Maxine Hong Kingston, Joy Kogawa* (Ithaca: Cornell University Press, 1993), p. 129.

12. Andrew Garrod, *Speaking for Myself: Canadian Writers in Interviews* (Breakwater Books, 1986), p. 140.

13. Peggy Phelan, *Mourning Sex: Performing Public Memories* (London: Routledge, 1997), p. 78.

14. Yamamoto, *op. cit.*, p. 105.

15. *Ibid.*, p. 106.

16. *Ibid.*, p. 122.

17. Smaro Kamboureli, *Scandalous Bodies: Diasporic Literature in English Canada* (Toronto: Oxford University Press, 2000), p. 197.

18. *Ibid.*

19. Marita Sturkin, *Tangled Memories: The Vietnam War, the AIDS Epidemic, and the Politics of Remembering* (Berkeley: University of California Press, 1997), p. 16.

20. Kamboureli, *op. cit.*, p. 188.

21. *Ibid.*, p. 206.

22. Joy Kogawa, *Obasan* (Toronto: Penguin, 1981), pp. 82-83.

23. Sturken, *op. cit.*, p. 5.

24. *Ibid.*, p. 1.

25. Cathy Caruth, *Trauma: Explorations in Memory* (Baltimore: Johns Hopkins University Press, 1995), p.5.

26. Palumbo-Liu, *op. cit.*, p. 393.

27. *Ibid.*, p. 388.

28. *Ibid.*. p. 389.

29. Caruth, *op. cit.*, p. vii).

30. *Ibid.*, p. 8.

31. *Ibid.*

32. *Ibid.*, p. 9.

33. *Ibid.*, p. 10.

34. *Ibid.*, p. 9.

35. *Ibid.*, p. 10.

36. *Ibid.*, p. 11.

SOCIAL AND POLITICAL STUDIES

WHEN THE GRASS IS NOT GREENER ON THE OTHER SIDE OR WHAT ITALIANS NEED TO KNOW ABOUT CANADA'S ELECTORAL SYSTEM

OSVALDO CROCI

1. Introduction

One of the many ongoing political debates in Italy concerns the reform of its proportional electoral system. First, a referendum held in 1991 abolished the preference vote, a feature thought to be responsible for electoral grafting and political corruption. Then, in August 1993, following a second referendum, a new electoral law was adopted. It set up a hybrid system providing for the election of three quarters of Parliament (both Senate and House of Commons) on a simple majoritarian basis, and one quarter on a proportional basis.[1] Finally, a referendum held on 18 April 1999 indicated that 91.5 per cent of voters favoured the abolition of the proportional component. However, the hybrid system remained in place because only 49.6 of those eligible exercised their right to vote, and thus the referendum failed to reach its necessary quorum of 50 per cent plus one.[2] In December 2005, Italy eliminated the majoritarian component of its electoral system and returned to a variation of the proportional system. The new system gives the party or coalition of parties which receives a plurality of votes 55% of the seats in the Chamber of Deputies. Parties and coalitions which receive less than 4 and 10 percent of the votes respectively will not receive any seats. It should be noted that the impetus behind the return to a proportional system was not the recognition of the limits of the simple majoritarian system but the fear of the Berlusconi-led centre right governing coalition that it might lose the elections of April 2006 under the hybrid system. Ironically, had the electoral system not been changed, the governing coalition would have been re-elected whereas with the new system it went down to defeat even if only to be returned to power again two years later.

While Italians are very familiar with the problems associated with a proportional electoral system, they know very little about those associated with the Single Member District Plurality System (henceforth SMDPS) that is used in Canada at both federal and provincial levels. Moreover, the debate on electoral reform has actually obfuscated rather than clarified the likely consequences the SMDPS would have in Italy. Thus, while Canadians have been considering for years some type of more proportional system,[3] Italians are very eager to adopt the SMDPS, and some of them even regard it as a panacea.

This chapter argues that, in relation to Italian expectations of the SMDPS, the grass is not necessarily greener on the Canadian side. It begins with a brief section on the role of electoral systems, then offers an illustration of the problems associated with the SMDPS in Canada, and advances a prediction of the consequences of the adoption of the SMDPS in Italy. It concludes with a reflection on the role played by the SMDPS in the framing of political discourse and choice.

2. Types of electoral systems

Electoral systems are mechanisms used to translate popular votes into parliamentary seats. They can be divided into two main types: proportional systems and majoritarian systems. Each of these types can be further divided into a number of sub-types. Proportional systems assign to each political party a percentage of parliamentary seats that is more or less proportional to the percentage of popular votes it receives. These systems are based on the principle that Members of Parliament (MPs) are spokespersons for societal interests, as aggregated and represented by political parties, on a national basis. The major consequence of proportional systems is that, in societies that exhibit numerous ethnic, economic, religious, or ideological cleavages, rarely is a political party able to win an absolute majority of the popular vote. As a result, majority governments (i.e. governments formed by one party enjoying the support of an absolute parliamentary majority) are a rare occurrence. Governments are usually formed by a coalition of two or more political parties. The major problem with coalition governments is that, because of disagreements, they tend to fall apart before their term comes to an end. Such has been the Italian experience, the current Berlusconi government being the 66th Italian government to take office since the fall of Mussolini in July 1943. Canada, on the other hand, has had only 23 governments since 1943.

The SMDPS is perhaps the most common type of majoritarian system. Unlike the proportional system, it is based on the principle of territorial representation, with each MP representing a specific electoral district.[4] The most important advantage of the SMDPS in a parliamentary regime is that, generally, although not necessarily, it results in the formation of one-party, majority governments because the SMDPS typically distorts the relationship between the percentage of popular vote a political party receives and the percentage of parliamentary seats the same party is allotted. Such a distortion generally, although again not necessarily, favours the party with the largest popular vote. In other words, this party usually receives a higher percentage of seats than the percentage of votes cast in its favour. The contrary is generally true for all other parties, except for those enjoying concentrated regional support.

3. Advantages of the SMDPS

3.1 Two-party systems

One reason Italians like the SMDPS is that its most enthusiastic proponents[5] have depicted it as being capable of reducing the number of political parties, thus leading to the formation of a two-party system. Yet, as argued by Duverger more than half a century ago, the formation of a two-party system, while favoured by the SMDPS, is not necessarily a consequence of its adoption.[6] Similarly, as shown by Rokkan, a proportional electoral system favours the formation of a multiparty system but does not create it. In some European countries, a multiparty system was in place well before the adoption of proportional electoral systems. The formation of multiparty systems was a consequence of universal suffrage. Social cleavages and not proportional electoral systems are at the origin of multiparty systems. Proportional systems simply favour and reproduce multiparty systems more than do majoritarian systems. Hence, in societies exhibiting many cleavages, multiparty systems might be the norm regardless of the type of electoral system those societies adopt.[7]

In Canada, for example, a two-party system ceased to exist in 1921 and, since 1935, at least four political parties have constantly been represented in Parliament: the Liberals, the Progressive Conservatives, the Cooperative Commonwealth Federation later renamed New Democratic Party, and the Social Credit. Although the latter disappeared in 1980, in the elections of 1993, following the formation of two new parties with a strong regional base, i.e. the Bloc Québécois and Reform, the parties represented in Parliament increased to five.

Hence, it is difficult to imagine how a SMDPS might lead to a two-party system in Italy where, besides traditional cleavages, regional ones are now politically significant. The partial adoption of the SMDPS in 1993 has undoubtedly favoured the bipolarization of the political system (i.e. political parties align for electoral purposes in two opposing camps) but bipolarization is something other than a two-party system. Bipolarization does not necessarily eliminate the need for coalitions. Rather negotiations to form coalitions take place before as opposed to after an election. This has significant advantages in that, for example, voters can punish or reward parties for their coalition choice, but it does not ensure that these new coalitions will last any longer than the old ones, as shown by the defection of the *Lega Nord* from the Berlusconi government in December 1994 and of *Rifondazione Comunista* from the Prodi government in 1998. The abandonment of the proportional system, moreover, actually increased the number of political parties. In a society where cleavages are strong, even if a two-party system could be created by decree, these cleavages would still find their way into the political arena even though only as factions within the two permitted parties.

3.2 Absolute majorities

Italians would also like to adopt the SMDPS because its proponents have suggested that it ensures parliamentary majorities to the party with the largest popular vote, even when this party wins only a relative majority of the vote. When one looks at the Canadian experience, however, the record on this point is, at best, mixed. As Table 1 shows, since 1921 there have been 24 elections in which the winning party won a relative majority of votes (i.e. received less than 50 per cent of the popular vote). In 11 of these 24 elections (i.e. in 45 percent of the cases), moreover, the winning party failed to gain an absolute majority of seats, the most notable failures occurring in six out of nine elections between 1957 and 1979 and the last three in 2004, 2006 and 2008. In these cases, in most parliamentary democracies coalition governments would be formed. Canada, however, seems to have a distaste for formal coalition governments and has relied instead on minority governments, i.e. governments formed by a party lacking a majority in the House of Commons but able nevertheless to win support from enough opposition members to avoid defeat on measures requiring a vote of confidence.[8]

4. Problems with the SMDPS

The previous analysis has shown that some of the advantages of the SMDPS appear to have been greatly exaggerated, e.g. the SMDPS does not necessarily lead to a two-party system nor does it consistently produce parliamentary majorities for one party. Furthermore, there are problems with the SMDPS which, although not mentioned in the Italian debate, explain why many Canadians are dissatisfied with this system.

4.1 Inequitable vote-seat conversion

As Table 1 shows, during the 27 federal elections between 1921 and 2008, the party that won an absolute majority of seats received an absolute majority of the popular vote only three times. The Liberals managed such a feat in 1940, whereas the Progressive Conservatives did so in 1958, and again in 1984. More often (81 percent of the cases), the party that won an absolute majority of seats did not receive the absolute majority of votes, which indicates that a majority of electors actually cast their vote against the party forming the majority government. This aspect of the SMDPS might not be of much interest to those who are tired of bickering and short-lived coalition governments and desire strong, long-lasting majority governments – and most Italians might indeed fall in this category. It should concern, however, all those citizens who believe that democracy means, first and foremost, rule by the party (or coalition) that has been endorsed by a majority of the electorate.

A related characteristic of the SMDPS is that the number of votes necessary to obtain a parliamentary seat is not the same for each party. As an example, in the last federal election, the Conservative party needed an average of about 35,000 votes for each seat, while the New Democratic Party needed an average of 67,000 votes. The Bloc Québécois, instead, needed an average of only about 28,000 votes. The type and degree of distortion between percentage of votes and seats depend primarily on the way electoral support for any given party is distributed geo-

graphically. Generally, except for the party winning a relative majority of votes that receives a "premium" in terms of
seats, all other parties are penalised unless they can count
on concentrated regional support. Sometimes, a modest
increase in the percentage of votes can lead to a dramatic
increase in the percentage of seats. In the 1976 Quebec
provincial elections, the Parti Québécois' share of the popular vote passed from 30 to 41 percent, while its number
of seats in the *Assemblée nationale* jumped from 6 to 71,
representing an increase of more than 1000 per cent. At
other times, a decrease in the percentage of votes may sig-
nify the disappearance or near-disappearance of the party
in the House of Commons. In the 1993 federal election,
the Progressive Conservatives lost 27 per cent of the popular vote (passing from 43 to 16 percent). Such a decrease
was undoubtedly significant but its consequences in terms
of seats were even more dramatic: the party lost all but 2
of its 169 seats, and went from being a one-party majority
government to losing even its party status in the House of
Commons (for which a minimum of 12 seats is required).

4.2 From "vote losers" to "seat winners"

Under the SMDPS it is not uncommon for the party with
the second-largest percentage of popular vote to win more
seats than the party with the largest percentage. In Canada,
this has happened three times in federal elections. As Table
1 shows, in 1957 the Liberals won 41 percent of the popular vote but obtained only 40 percent of the seats, while
the Progressive Conservatives obtained 42 percent of the
seats with 39 percent of the votes. In 1962, the Liberals
won 37.4 percent of the popular vote, while the
Progressive Conservatives won 37.3 percent. However,

whereas the Progressive Conservatives won 44 percent of the seats, the Liberals won only 38 percent. The Progressive Conservatives fared even better in 1979 when they won 36 percent of the popular vote but managed to obtain 48 percent of the seats. The Liberals, who had won 40 percent of the popular vote, had to content themselves with 40 percent of the seats. In Canadian provincial elections, the "wrong party", i.e. the "vote loser", became the "seat winner" on eight different occasions: in Saskatchewan in 1986 and 1999, in Quebec in 1966 and 1998, in British Columbia in 1952 and 1996, in New Brunswick in 1974, and in Newfoundland in 1989.

4.3 The opposition

In their desire to form parliamentary majorities, citizens should not forget that a key characteristic of a democracy is the protection it gives to the opposition. Under the SMDPS, the representation of the opposition and minorities in general can be severely weakened because non-winning parties usually receive a smaller percentage of seats than they would in a proportional system. In some cases, the SMDPS can actually eliminate the opposition, which does little to promote the democratic exercise of power. At the provincial level, this has happened twice: in Prince Edward Island in 1935, and in New Brunswick in 1987. In both cases, it was the provincial Liberal party that won all the seats. The Liberals came close to repeating the feat in P.E.I. in 1993, when they won 31 seats out of 32. In the April 2000 election, the situation was reversed, the Conservatives winning 26 of the 27 now available in the provincial assembly.

4.4 *Regionalization of parties*

The SMDPS also promotes the "regionalization" of political parties. This phenomenon manifests itself in two ways. First, the SMDPS favours those parties whose support is concentrated in one region and penalises parties whose support is more evenly distributed across the country. As Table 2 shows, the SMDPS has generally treated more favourably the Social Credit whose support was concentrated in the Western provinces, than the New Democrats whose support has traditionally been more evenly spread across the country. The same is true for the Bloc Québécois when compared to the New Democrats, the Progressive Conservatives in the elections of 1993, 1997 and 2000, and even to Reform/Canadian Alliance, which was primarily a Western party but with considerable support in Ontario.

In 1997, the Bloc Québécois won a higher number and percentage of seats than did the Progressive Conservatives, even if it received a lower percentage of votes. This success was due to the fact that its support was concentrated in the province of Quebec. In fact, the Bloc does not run candidates anywhere else. The same was generally true for Reform Party which had its support concentrated in the West. The New Democrats are instead generally penalized by the fact that party's support is more evenly spread across the country.

"Regionalization" also refers to the identification that a party acquires with a region of the country. Party images are primarily a function of their parliamentary strength and not of their popular support in the country. The New Democrats are considered a minor party simply because they obtain only about half of the seats they would receive under a proportional system. The Liberals have acquired an anti-Western image (at least since 1957) because the party has elected very few MPs west of Ontario even if it normally receives over 20 per cent of the popular vote in the Western provinces. The Progressive Conservatives were rarely able to elect candidates in Quebec until 1984. As a consequence, the party acquired a non-French, or even anti-French, image in spite of the fact that it regularly won an average of 13% of the votes in that province. Finally, the Reform Party/Canadian Alliance had a Western image because almost all of its MPs were elected in the Western provinces. Yet, in the 2000 election, the party received over 24 per cent of the vote in Ontario, 16 per cent in New Brunswick, and 10 per cent in Nova Scotia.

It seems fair to conclude that, at least in the Canadian experience, the SMDPS has had a "centrifugal" influence on the national polity. The SMDPS, by "regionalizing" political parties, instead of providing a solution to the problem of national disintegration – political parties are, after all, reputed to be one of the most important factors of national integration – has made this problem more severe. In the Italian context, the SMDPS would probably have the same "regionalizing" effects on parties: it would increase the number of seats won by the *Lega Nord* (a milder Italian version of the Bloc Québécois) in its strongholds of the Venetian northeast and northern Lombardy. At the same time, it would penalize, or even eliminate, all the small parties that cannot rely on strong regional support. Finally, the SMDPS would emphasize the already existing "regional" image of the two parties: the *Popolo della Libertà* would be perceived, somewhat contradictorily as both a northern and southern party while the *Partito Democratico* would be identified as the party of central Italy. Rather than facilitating the task of governing the country (what the Italians call *governabilità*), the adoption of the SMDPS would most likely worsen the centrifugal processes already at work.

4.5 From politics to administration

The debate on electoral reform in Italy rarely mentions the shortcomings of the SMDPS. This is probably due not exclusively to a lack of awareness of their existence but also to the fact that the SMDPS is advocated for reasons other than those openly mentioned. *Governabilità* does not only refer to the ability to form a majority government. Even if rarely admitted, the term also refers to the desire to reduce the ideological spectrum of political parties to simple variants of the same liberal ideology, and thus restrict political choice by eliminating all radical alternatives.

Seen from this perspective, the adoption of the SMDPS would serve a very important function. Even in countries with a relatively large ideological spectrum such as Italy, the electorate distributes itself according to a bell shaped curve, i.e. most voters, and especially the volatile group that often decides elections, are concentrated in the median position. This means that, under the SMDPS, parties are forced to converge towards the centre of the ideological spectrum unless they are willing to accept a permanently marginal position at the opposition. The SMDPS therefore has the ability to transform the political debate into a technical-administrative one. What is discussed and what has to be chosen are no longer different models of society but slightly different technical alternatives within the same model of liberal society. Under these conditions, the non-liberal parties (i.e. parties that do not subscribe to the liberal ideology) capable of gaining representation in Parliament, and only at the opposition, are primarily those that are capable of developing regionally concentrated support, which they usually do by claiming that the interests of that region are ignored by the central government. In other words, the SMDPS has a centripetal effect on the ideological spectrum of political parties, and a centrifugal one on the national polity. Both processes are already at work in Italy. While the *Popolo della Libertà* advocates the rule of the market and a smaller and unobtrusive government (classic liberalism), the *Partito Democratico* promotes a vision of society in which the harsher consequences of the market are mitigated by a more socially active government (welfare liberalism). In terms of the policies they advance, these two parties are already the Italian replica of the Conservative Party and the Liberals, respectively. The only party that would survive outside these two is the *Lega*, a regionally based party. The SMDPS would de-emphasise class politics, or capital versus labour, and emphasise instead territorial politics: East versus West in Canada, and North against South in Italy.

5. Conclusion

This brief discussion of the consequences of the SMDPS in Canada suggests that Italians may wish to reconsider their expectations. The SMDPS might lead to more solid and, therefore, more lasting majority governments. Nonetheless, its adoption could possibly create new, but not less serious, problems. There is no perfect electoral system. Each system simply maximizes certain values to the detriment of others. Everything else being equal, the proportional system privileges fairness in representation but risks producing weak and short-lived executives. The SMDPS is more effective at producing majority governments but weakens, or even completely suppresses, the voice of some sectors of society while amplifying that of regionally based groups. At first glance, the SMDPS may appear to be a preferable system to Italians because they know all too well problems associated with the proportional system. In light of the Canadian experience with the SMDPS, Italians are well advised to reconsider their expectations: the grass is not necessarily greener on the Canadian side.

Notes

1. Simon Parker, "Electoral reform and political change in Italy, 1991-1994" in Stephen Gundle and Simon Parker (eds.), *The New Italian Republic: from the fall of the Berlin wall to Berlusconi*, London and New York: Routledge, 1996, pp. 40-56.

2. Mark Donovan, "The end of Italy's referendum anomaly?" in Mark Gilbert and Gianfranco Pasquino (eds.), *Italian Politics: the faltering transition*, Oxford and New York: Berghahn Books, 2001, pp. 51-66.

3. The debate on electoral reform in Canada began in the late 1960s with the seminal article by Alan Cairns, "The electoral system and the party system in Canada" *Canadian Journal of Political Science*, March 1968, pp. 55-80. For later contributions to this debate, see: William Irvine, *Does Canada need a new electoral system?* Kingston: Institute for Intergovernmental Relations, 1979; Henry Milner (ed.), *Making every vote count: reassessing Canada's electoral system*, Peterborough: Broadview Press, 1999; Dennis Pilon, *Canada's Democratic Deficit: Is Proportional Representation the Answer?* Toronto: The CSJ Foundation for Research and Education, 2000; Judy Rebick and Walter Robinson, "We vote to scrap the system" *The Globe and Mail*, November 29, 2000, p. A19.

4. One could of course discuss at length whether this type of representation makes sense in modern democratic societies, but this is not the focus of this essay.

5. These include politicians such as Giuseppe Calderisi, Mariotto Segni, Marco Pannella, and Augusto Barbera. The arguments of the latter can be found in his book *Una riforma per la Repubblica*, Roma: Editori Riuniti, 1991.

6. Maurice Duverger, *Political Parties*, London: Methuen, 1954.

7. Stein Rokkan, *Citizens, Elections, Parties*, New York: McKay, 1970.

8. On minority governments in Canada see Peter H. Russell, *Two cheers for minority governments. The evolution of Canadian parliamentary democracy*, Toronto: Emond Montgomery, 2008.

Comparison of percentage of popular vote and
percentage of seats for federal elections, 1921-2000.

Year	L Vote	L Seats	PC Vote	PC Seats	NDP Vote	NDP Seats	CA Vote	CA Seats	BQ Vote	BQ Seats
1921	41	49	30	21						
1925	40	40	46	47						
1926	46	52	45	37						
1930	45	37	49	56						
1935	45	71	30	16	9	3				
1940	52	74	31	16	9	3				
1945	41	51	27	27	16	11				
1949	49	74	30	16	13	5				
1953	49	64	31	19	11	9				
1957	41	40	39	42	11	9				
1958	34	18	54	79	10	3				
1962	37	38	37	44	14	7				
1963	42	49	33	36	13	6				
1965	40	49	33	36	18	8				
1968	45	58	31	27	17	8				
1972	38	41	35	40	18	12				
1974	43	53	33	37	20	11				
1979	40	40	36	48	18	9				
1980	44	52	33	37	20	11				
1984	28	14	50	75	19	11				
1988	32	28	43	57	20	15				
1993	41	60	16	1	7	3	19	18	13	18
1997	38	52	19	7	11	7	19	20	11	15
2000	41	58	12	4	9	4	25	22	11	12

Source: Rand Dyck, *Canadian Politics*, 3rd edition (Scarborough: Nelson, 2000), p. 266.
Note: L refers to Liberal; PC refers to Conservative and its successor Progressive
Conservative; NDP refers to the NDP and its predecessor, the CCF; CA refers to
Canadian Alliance and its predecessor, Reform; BQ refers to Bloc Québécois.

Ratio between % of seats and % of popular vote by party for federal election, 1921-2009

Year	LP	PC/CP	NDP	SC	RP/CA	BQ
1921	1.2	0.7				
1925	1	1.02				
1926	1.1	0.82				
1930	0.8	1.14				
1935	1.6	0.53	0.3			
1940	1.4	0.51	0.3			
1945	1.2	1	0.7	1.29		
1949	1.5	0.53	0.4	1.03		
1953	1.3	0.61	0.8	1.06		
1957	1	1.07	0.8	1.09		
1958	0.5	1.46	0.3	#		
1962	1	1.18	0.5	0.97		
1963	1.2	1.09	0.5	0.76		
1965	1.2	1.09	0.4	0.51*		
1968	1.3	0.87	0.5	1.21		
1972	1.1	1.14	0.7	0.75		
1974	1.2	1	0.4	0.82		
1979	1	1.33	0.5	0.46		
1980	1.2	1.12	0.6			
1984	0.5	1.5	0.6			
1988	0.9	1.32	0.8			
1993	1.5	0.05	0.4		0.94	1.4
1997	1.4	0.35	0.6		1.04	1.4
2000	1.4	0.33	0.4		0.88	1.1
2004	1.2	1.06	0.4			1.4
2006	1.1	1.11	0.5			1.6
2008	1.1	1.11	0.5			1.6

2.7% of the votes, no seats
*Presented a separate ticket in Québec.

Percentage of popular vote, number of seats and percentage of seats by province, federal elections 1997 and 2008

		L			PC/CP			NDP			RP			BQ		
		%v	ns	%s	%v	ns	%s	%v	ns	%s	%v	ns	%s	%v	ns	%s
NF (7)	1997	38	4	57	37	3	43	22	0	0	3	0	0			
-7	2008	47	6	86	17	0	0	34	1	14						
PEI (4)	1997	45	4	100	38	0	0	15	0	0	2	0	0			
-4	2008	48	3	75	36	1	25	10	0	0						
NS (11)	1997	28	0	0	31	5	45	30	6	55	10	0	0			
(11)*	2008	30	5	46	26	3	27	29	2	18						
NB (10)	1997	33	3	30	35	5	50	18	2	20	13	0	0			
-10	2008	32	3	30	39	6	60	22	1	10						
QU (75)	1997	37	26	35	22	5	7	2	0	0	0.3	0	0	38	44	58
(75)*	2008	24	14	19	22	10	13	12	1	1				38	49	65
ON (103)	1997	50	101	98	19	1	1	11	0	0	19	0	0			
-106	2008	34	38	36	39	51	48	18	17	16						
MN (14)	1997	34	6	43	18	1	7	23	4	29	24	3	21			
-15	2008	19	1	7	49	9	64	24	4	29						
SK (14)	1997	25	1	7	8	0	0	31	5	36	36	8	57			
-14	2008	15	1	7	54	13	93	26	0	0						
AB (26)	1997	24	2	8	14	0	0	6	0	0	55	24	92			
-28	2008	11	0	0	65	27	96	13	1	4						
BC (34)	1997	29	6	18	6	0	0	19	3	9	43	25	73			
-36	2000	19	5	14	44	22	61	26	9	25						
NWT (2)	1997	43	2	100	17	0	0	21	0	0	14	0	0			
-1	2008	14	0	0	38	0	0	42	1	1						
YU (1)	1997	22	0	0	14	0	0	29	1	100	26	0	0			
-1	2008	45	1	100	33	0	0	9	0	0						
NUN (1)	2008	29	0	0	35	1	100	28	0	0						

* One independent elected in each of Nova Scotia and Quebec
Source: Elections Canada.

CANADIAN TRADITION
AND AMERICAN REVOLUTION

Bruce Clark, Aboriginal Rights,
and Neo-Liberalism in Canada

ROBIN MATHEWS

The forces pushing Canada toward and pulling it away
from the U.S.A. are probably buried in the psyche of every
Canadian. For some, merely to say "Canada and the
U.S.A." is to declare a dialectic, the two poles of which
bespeak ineradicable differences definitive of the two communities. Those differences are very often summed up in
key words – what one might call slogan words – for the
Canada/U.S.A. dialectic is almost always brought to consciousness in arguments and debates at which times signs
and symbols – the semiotics of whole patterns of thought –
are invoked. Two key words involved are "tradition" and
"revolution" and they sum up fundamental aspects of the
two societies. One may argue that the U.S. "War for
Independence" can only be called a "revolution" by the
most romantic of thinkers. But the war effected the rend-
ing of a continuous fabric, without doubt. The "continuous
fabric" remained in what we call Canada, which is one significant reason why the "tradition" side of the dialectic
remains with us.

In a truly fascinating confrontation of forces which are

intimately involved with Native rights in Canada, Bruce Clark has lifted into the light a fundamental, traditional and seemingly incontrovertible proof – often disguised, obfuscated, opportunistically denied, even militantly rejected – for Native claims to territory and to independent government that lie wholly within the rule of law and the constitutional structure of Canada, in short, based upon the real and deeply meaningful "tradition" of this place.[1] Clark's achievement has been to cut through endless obfuscation and lay bare a constitutional and legal argument of great power. I do not intend to argue with other theories; that would require a book. Suffice it to say that Brian Slattery's overall theory of aboriginal rights as continuous fabric seems, in general, to support Clark's thesis.[2] Peter Kulchyski, on the other hand, claiming that it is important to stress "the ways in which Aboriginal rights were ignored 'from early colonial days'" doesn't seem to add anything to the debate.[3] That is because anyone who argues for the continuous fabric in constitutional and legal terms has to take for granted that the argument is news to a great many judges, governments, and legal practitioners in our time.

Within Canada, as within the individual Canadian psyche, a dialectic exists between what we think of as U.S. values and the values arising out of the uniquely Canadian tradition. That so strong and punitive resistance to Clark's findings has been mounted (including the act of disbarring him from practicing law) reflects the present vitality of neo-liberalism at almost every level of power in the country.

The term "neo-liberalism" means, for the purposes of this discussion, market individualism, individualism removed from the checks, balances and modifications that the community has evolved over time. It means, as must follow, the rejection – on behalf of the instruments of instantaneous gratification – of the terms of law and behaviour set up by tradition. Neo-liberalism involves a rejection of the rule of law historically enunciated on behalf of the rule of men holding sufficient power to work their will, even if they do so by passing so-called "laws" based on apparently majoritarian wishes. In Canada, it means the unburdening of federal powers (and responsibilities, including the responsibility for Native rights) and their distribution to the regions which can, in effect, remake them as part of powerfully destructive revisionisms. It means, finally, a definition of the human person that is not only based upon individual rights before community rights, but, as a corollary, the right (rarely admitted by the proponents of individual rights) to the exaction of inequalities made possible by power alone. Neo-Liberalism often masquerades as the ultimate embodiment of equality when it is the categorical denial of equality, for it exalts the individual's right to take a position superior in power to his or her fellows and to profit from that power. Very briefly, the U.S.A. as a state exercises that kind of exaction with such consistency in world affairs that people accept it as given. Indeed, the "U.S. global policeman," for instance, frequently operates outside any recognizable rule of law or any fundamental belief in human equality, whatever rhetoric it employs to mask its lawless actions.

To place the argument within a Canada/U.S.A. dialectic might seem far-fetched to some, except – quite simply – the claim of Native right made in Canada cannot be made in the U.S.A. where "revolution" changed the definition, role and powers of the Native people despite a legal history laced with ringing declarations of Indian rights.[4]

That set of facts is so important to this discussion that it must briefly be characterized. The differences between the U.S.A. and Canada on basic Native status make and have made a significant difference in history. Perhaps four facts provide terms with which to work. First, the *Royal Proclamation* of 1763 set out the right of Natives not to be "molested or disturbed" upon unceded lands. Because we will be referring to the *Royal Proclamation* throughout, we will quote the relevant passage:

> And whereas it is just and reasonable, and essential to our interest, and the Security of our Colonies, that the several Nations or Tribes of Indians with whom We are connected and who live under our Protection, should not be molested or disturbed in the Possession of such Parts of Our Dominions and Territories as, not having been ceded to or purchased by Us, are reserved to them, or any of them, as their Hunting Grounds. We do therefore, with the Advice of our Privy Council, declare it our Royal Will and Pleasure, that no Governor or Commander in Chief in any of our Colonies of Quebec, East Florida, or West Florida, do presume, upon any Pretence whatever, to grant Warrants of Survey, or pass any Patents for any Lands beyond the Heads or Sources of any of the Rivers which fall into the Atlantic Ocean from the West and North West, or upon any Lands whatever, which, not having been ceded to or purchased by Us as aforesaid are reserved to the said Indians or any of them.

> And, We do further strictly enjoin and require all Persons whatever who have either willfully or inadvertently seated themselves upon any Lands within the Countries above described, or upon any other Lands which , not having been ceded to or purchased by Us are still reserved for the said Indians as aforesaid forthwith to remove themselves from such Settlements.

> And whereas great Frauds and Abuses have been committed in purchasing Lands of the Indians, to the great Prejudice of our interests, and to the great Dissatisfaction of the said Indians; In order, therefore, to prevent such irregularities for the future, and to the end that the Indians may be convinced of our Justice and determined Resolution to remove all reasonable Cause of Discontent, We do, with the Advice of our Privy Council strictly enjoin and require, that if at any Time any of the Said Indians should be inclined to dispose of the said Lands the same shall be Purchased only for Us in our Name at some public Meeting or Assembly of the said Indians.[5]

The only negotiator who could treat with the Indian peoples for sale of unceded lands was proclaimed to be the Crown which was required to follow a clear process in such cases. The Proclamation was made before the U.S. Declaration of Independence in 1776 and so it applied to what we may call "the U.S. colonies." Not only did secession of the U.S.A. from British power permit a reconstruction of those Native rights but, secondly, an ugly precedent intervened. Many people who supported the rebelling forces in the War for Independence were rewarded with grants of unceded Indian land seized without due process. And so whatever high-sounding claims U.S. judges could and would make in succeeding generations, a precedent lay that Indian land had been seized; and it had been used by central power to pay allies and friends at the very outset of the life of the United States.

Thirdly, the *Royal Proclamation* was a contributing factor among the motivations for the War for Independence. It was not the only factor. In the (U.S.) colonies deep antagonism was raised over British maritime laws which strictly regulated marine trade, for instance. But the *Royal Proclamation* demanded a clearly visible rule of law for the acquisition of Indian lands, an idea that was simply anathema to many white settlers, land brokers, and theorists of U.S. aggrandizement. Fourthly, the *Quebec Act* of 1774 granted the francophones enduring rights and confirmed boundaries of their territory southward. Settlers in what we now call the U.S.A., says *The Canadian Encyclopedia*, "were enraged when Quebec acquired Indian territory, which they perceived to be theirs by right; they considered the Quebec Act one of the 'Intolerable Acts' which contributed to the outbreak of the American Revolution."[6] More lay behind the *Quebec Act*, however, than is suggested in that quotation. The (U.S.) colonies were determined from very early times to eradicate francophone power in North America. As early as 1709, a grand plan for the extirpation of French power was drawn up in the colonies to add to the unrelenting pressure upon England to act. And so the legitimation of the francophone colonists in 1774, in itself, enraged (U.S.) colonials. Indeed, Fred Anderson, in *Crucible of War*, claims the battle by the (U.S.) colonists against British imperialism was fundamentally imperialistic itself.[7] In his review of Anderson's book, Michael Rose points out that "it was the limitation of westward expansion beyond the Allegheny Mountains imposed on them by the British that lay at the core of the opposition by the powerful settlers and land speculators of North America to British rule."[8] The taxation question – which is often the one presented to popular audiences as a major reason for the War for Independence – was real enough. But much more of the taxation being demanded from the (U.S.) colonies was to be used for defence of their frontiers from Indian incursions about which the colonials complained constantly.

Perhaps it is not irrelevant in the face of later U.S. actions to remark that during the civil disturbances before the War for Independence, the (U.S.) colonists very often used mob tactics, organized violence and coercion against courts and authorities, often in the defence of piracy. Later, the rule of law was to some degree present in the expansion of the U.S.A. But the "Wild West" (the lawless expansion) was real, and it was preceded – a good deal more than is perceived – by a "Wild East." That fact is important for finding precedent for the "Wild West" and for understanding the racial extermination tactics carried out against the Indian people of the U.S.A. The U.S.A. was engaged in imperialistic expansionism long before generally recognized – and that imperialism was little interested in taking prisoners. The U.S.A. was founded, we must remember, in the same year as the publication of Adam Smith's *The Wealth of Nations*, the text that has become the sacred document of neo-liberalism; the "Wild East" and the "Wild West" were both tendencies in the U.S.A. as it took up Adam Smith as its new prophet. As Bruce Clark writes in the first sentence of his "Introduction" to *Indian Title in Canada*: "Law and practice represent two different, and sometimes opposed, perspectives on aboriginal rights."[9]

One of the paramount characteristics of U.S.A. "exceptionalism" was shaped very early by that split: the pursuit of U.S.A. Manifest Destiny frequently used law as the decoration upon violent, lawless and inhumane practices. That is a subject that deserves close attention in relation to black slavery as well as the treatment of Indians.

But the discussion here is concerned with the structures of aboriginal history in Canada to which the U.S.A. experience provides a fitting and important comparison. Bruce Clark, in that regard, worked over a long period of time and, as I have written above, lifted into the light a fundamental, traditional, and seemingly incontrovertible proof for Native claims to territory and independent government that lie wholly within the rule of law and the constitutional structure of Canada, a continuous fabric unbroken by war, revolution or imperial aspirations.

A few words about Bruce Clark are necessary, for he is central to the discussion, and he will be seen, increasingly as time passes, to be central to that fundamental argument about the Native peoples in Canada, their power, and their place in Canadian society.

Born in Kenora of fairly mixed origins, his father drowned when Clark was a small boy in the middle 1940s. He and his mother moved to Whitehorse where she put

him in a residential school at five years of age. Though he
had a little Indian in his background, apparently, Clark was
not an Indian and, as he says of his time at the residential
school: "I was there because it happened to be available."
Indeed, he reports that his mother "never expressed any
animosity towards natives. They were simply marginal to
her existence."[10] He felt despair at the school, though not
from any serious mistreatment. He makes the observation
that even those Natives (elsewhere) who were seriously
mistreated suffered most from a sense of powerlessness and
a lack of respect.

He and his mother left Whitehorse for Sudbury where
he was educated from Grade 4 to the age of nineteen. He
completed a law degree at the University of Western
Ontario, wanted to do mixed legal work in a small place,
and went to Haileybury in Northern Ontario. By the time
he was twenty-nine, he was a small-town lawyer doing the
normal work of such a place with, perhaps, the exception
that an Indian population was present and legal work
sometimes involved people from that population.

I have quickly summarized nearly the first thirty years
of Bruce Clark's life because it is not remarkably different
from the lives of many others, though it had tragedies and
stresses in it, and it involved close relations with Native
people. He was early aware of justice in relation to himself
and others. He tended to bridle when asked to conform,
but that, too, is not very remarkable in the young.

He did the job of lawyer in a small place without serious misgivings or feelings of alienation. Bruce Clark, I
believe, crossed the "great divide" of his life in 1973 when
the Temagamis of Bear Island asked him to represent them
in an effort to defend their native sovereignty. The set of
events that attached to and followed that request changed
Clark's life in a number of ways. As far, probably, as he is

concerned, it set him on the road to ostracism from the legal community and it moved him to become an elegant expert on aboriginal history and law.

For the rest of us the importance of the change is, I suppose, also at least twofold. Clark discovered the power of the courts to do wrong and he followed a path of research that permitted him the opportunity to present a case for the integrity of Native claims over unceded lands in Canada, a claim so telling and insistent that courts have refused so far to hear the argument. At that point – the point at which the courts resolutely refuse to discuss the question of their jurisdiction to hear cases involving aboriginal title – we enter the pervasive milieu of neo-liberalism. We will examine the reason they refuse, and comment upon their unsuitability to hear arguments involving aboriginal title. But first, a little more history, legal and political.

The Temagamis of Bear Island had never signed a treaty, and so dwelled on land unceded to the Crown. What is more, their land is dense with rock-painting sites marking a sacred area. Not only was the Ontario government planning to build a large ski resort on a sacred mountain of the Temagamis, but it helped create increased pollution in the area from the Sudbury smelting operations. Timber companies wanted the remaining red and white pine of the area and open-pit mining was desecrating the hillsides. Acid rain was threatening fish, lakes and soil. A dilemma confronting Bruce Clark was one from which he has never been able to escape. The Temagamis had never ceded their land. They were, then, as subsequent examination will show, an entity which was in important ways outside the jurisdiction of Canadian courts. That is an enormous statement and must be very carefully explained. If some argue that they *were* within that jurisdiction, they must account for the facts that the courts resolutely refused to grant that any argument could exist on the basis of the lands unceded by the Temagamis had a specific existence outside the reach of the courts.

Put simply, the land of Canada was in part conquered and in part integrated without military action into the Empire of the British Crown. To begin, the Conquest was of the French who ceded their rights to the country to the British. The Conquest was not of the Native people, and the British made that fact very clear. From the beginning, as the *Royal Proclamation* declared, lands occupied by the Indians were carefully protected. The British recognized that land not purchased from "Indian nations" remained theirs to use or dispose of. They could not be disposed of to any other party but the Crown, nor could the Canadian government claim the land without a treaty concluded by a process quite clearly set out. That condition has never been changed in law.[11] In 1887, with regard to the case *R. v. St. Catherines Milling & Lumber Co.*, Mr. Justice Strong of the Supreme Court of Canada remarked upon the reasons for the *Royal Proclamation* and its effect:

> Its true origin was, I take it, experience of the great impolicy of the opposite mode of dealing with the Indians which had been practised by some of the Provincial governments of the older colonies and which had led to frequent frontier wars, involving great sacrifices of life and property and requiring an expenditure of money which had proved most burdensome to the colonies. That the more liberal treatment accorded to the Indians by this system of protecting them in the enjoyment of their hunting grounds and prohibiting settlement on land which they had not surrendered was successful in its results, is attested by the historical fact that from the memorable year 1763, when Detroit was beseiged and all the Indian tribes were in revolt, down to the date of confederation, Indian wars and massacres entirely ceased in the British possessions of North America, although powerful Indian nations still continued for some time after the former date to inhabit those territories. That this peaceful con-

duct of the Indians is in a great degree to be attributed to the recognition of their rights to lands unsurrendered by them, and to the guarantee of their protection in the possession and enjoyment of such lands given by the crown in the proclamation of October, 1763 is a well known fact of Canadian history which cannot be controverted.[12]

Very clearly, Mr. Justice Strong is reiterating the fact, in 1887, that the vitality of the *Royal Proclamation* of 1763 was continuous Canadian law.

Incidentally, a treaty – especially at the time of the Indian treaties – was primarily a formally signed agreement between states in their international relations. In the *Encylopaedia Britannica* of both 1771 (three volumes, first edition) and 1797 (eighteen volumes, third edition), for instance, the definition of treaty given is simply "a covenant between two or more nations; or the several articles or conditions stipulated and agreed upon by two sovereign powers." Thus, to take an Indian entity holding unceded land (i.e., land that has never been purchased by the Crown through treaty) into a Canadian court in order to settle a grievance about land is to go before a court of the state with which one is in conflict, and such a court will be, by definition, a biased agency. In addition, it is to acknowledge that the Canadian court somehow has jurisdiction, somehow has the power to dispose of the dispute as it would between two parties arguing, say, over the ownership of a private company. It is to say, in effect, that the dispute is *not* between two entities equal in law, both possessing sovereignty that neither, in the case, is subservient to the other or to the other's judicial system, and therefore requires a third party adjudicator. It is to assume that the judge, appointed to the court and paid for by one party to the dispute, belonging to the culture and the sovereignty of that party, may fairly adjudicate between his or her "master" and the party with which the master is in dispute. To put it yet another way, it is as if a judge were to adjudicate between two parties arguing over the ownership of a private company when one of the parties was not only paying his salary but accepted him as one of its party in seeking ownership.

The dilemma faced by Bruce Clark was, in brief, that the act of going before a Canadian court with the Temagami grievance was a declaration of defeat on the fundamental matter of jurisdiction, a matter of primary importance since justice, by definition, could not be achieved from a biased adjudicator, though Clark was still – at that time – willing to believe impartial adjudication was possible from the Canadian courts. To complicate the matter, the Temagamis, themselves, had concluded and they believed that their own court had jurisdiction. During his early work for the Temagamis when he was, in fact, supporting their case from his own funds and had entered a very effective "caution" blocking development of their lands, a completely coincidental force (we are invited to believe) entered the picture without, of course, having any relation to the legal position he had taken and the work he was doing. He was visited by representatives of the Canadian Income Tax Department, Revenue Canada, who told him that, if he didn't start paying his tax arrears without delay, they would begin what would be in fact the garnishment of his "wages." They would inform all of his clients to make payments owing Clark directly to Revenue Canada. The representatives from Revenue Canada knew and he knew the action would destroy his business. He unburdened himself of his clientele, moved to Bear Island, and continued his work for the Natives.

It seems that in Clark's *Indian Title in Canada* he came to believe in the existence of a secondary level of sovereignty, "domestic sovereignty," which was possessed by the Native peoples. That excluded them from the quality of nationhood that would empower them to engage in foreign treaty making or other such acts as they were "taken" as part of the British imperial holding. But it did not suggest they were amenable to the jurisdiction of an "interested" court, even when that court's powers derived, at least in part, from the Royal power that gave them their special protection. And that is because the "interested" court (the Canadian court) was no longer pure arbitrator as the monarch had been.

The monarch in the *Royal Proclamation* of 1763 chose to stand between the Native peoples and those with designs upon their lives and territories, *very clearly* whether they were governments or private parties. Proof of that was discovered by Clark in the judgement made concerning the *Mohegan Indians v. Connecticut*, decided (after nearly seventy years of litigation) by the Privy Council in 1773, ten years after the *Royal Proclamation* and three years before the U.S. Declaration of Independence. In that connection Clark writes significantly: "such appeals included questions of political jurisdiction and not just private law questions involving disputes in litigated matters."[13] In the case the Privy Council ruled the Indians could not sustain their argument that they had granted their lands to the colony so that it could hold them in trust for them. But the legitimacy of the case was upheld on the ground that the Mohegans were "a quasi-sovereign nation."[14] Clark comments in a footnote: "The point is not that the Indian nations were 'foreign,' but rather that they were sovereign in the same way that the colonial governments were sovereign – that is, vested with a delimited jurisdiction independent of all other governments except as against the imperial government."[15] The courts of Canada subsequently (after Confederation) claim the right to adjudicate between the Native peoples and those who have designs upon their lives and territories, but the courts of Canada have no legal act of separation from the *Royal Proclamation*, subsequent rulings and developments from it. That places them, in their present role, in an invidious condition for they cannot exist as anything but parties intrinsic to, and/or in essence indistinguishable from the federal or governments doing the *designing* (since private parties cannot litigate in the matter). When Native people go before the Supreme Court of Canada for a judgement on matters of land or aboriginal powers, it is as if the Mohegans went before the highest court of Connecticut with their grievance. The judges who preside over the courts of Canada are appointed and paid by government; and the maintenance and operation of the courts are the responsibility of those governments. So, when any Native person appears or when a number of Native people appear before any court of Canada on a matter of the status of lands and of aboriginal powers, the Native entity is appearing before *a tainted adjudicator*.

That, too, is an enormous statement and must be very carefully explained. At Confederation the Government of Canada took over the imperial responsibility for Native people without any change whatsoever in their status. In addition, no constitutional change has ever been enacted to restructure Native rights. It goes without saying that no political event like the War for Independence between Britain and the U.S.A. severed the continuous fabric of Canadian law. For those reasons, Canadian courts are absolutely under obligation to respond to the full meaning of the *Royal Proclamation* of 1763, to full recognition of the meaning of unceded lands. They do not and, what is more, they have so far refused to consider that the nature of their manifest and almost unbroken bias demands full examination in terms of their claim to jurisdiction as impartial adjudicators.

The question of "domestic sovereignty" may cause a reader difficulty. What is it? Clark suggests its basis in *Indian Title in Canada*, writing of what we think of as a sovereign nation: "The supreme authority in an independent political society in international terms," he writes, "it is nevertheless limited internally by the constitutional premises which define the society."[16] The limits are a portion of the society's constitutional definition and "domestic sovereignty" describes a large part of those limits. We recognize the principle easily in Canadian society because the "division of powers" in Canadian Confederation has, from the beginning, granted certain *exclusive* powers to the provinces, meaning powers that may not be infringed upon by the federal government ("the supreme authority in an independent political society in international terms") without negotiation and agreement by the province or provinces concerned. By the same token, on the unceded lands of Canada, domestic sovereignty is possessed by the political entities called "the several Nations or Tribes of Indians with whom we are connected [who] should not be molested or disturbed in the possession of such Parts of Our Dominions and Territories as not having been ceded or purchased by Us are reserved to them or any of them."[17] In Canada, a country in which the provinces guard their exclusive powers (their domestic sovereignty) tenaciously, it is perhaps ironic that they should be blind to the fact of another level of domestic sovereignty, the domestic sovereignty held by Native peoples over unceded land. Indeed, following in an unbroken thread (the continuous tradition) from the *Royal Proclamation* of 1763 until this moment, the Native peoples have exclusive powers, "existing aboriginal and treaty rights" (s. 35, *Constitution Act*, 1982).

The difficulty is that no court in Canada is willing fully to entertain those rights.

An argument certainly lies that the *Royal proclamation* expresses an assumption by the British Imperial government that is without foundation and that the Native peoples are not domestically sovereign but are sovereign without any encumbrance whatsoever. The argument is that when Europeans "found" North America, it had not been "lost" by the inhabitants. Having "come upon it" provided no meaningful basis for the Europeans to say, "this is ours." So one may go to the time anterior to European arrival on this continent and the *Royal Proclamation* and argue that the Native people were sovereign, but were pushed aside, violated, and had their land seized by various arriving European interests. The violations and removals engaged in by the Europeans did not provide a right to extinguish Native sovereignty. If the argument of right from "coming upon" (discovery) fails, it is because it may be seen as a huge façade erected by European triumphalism to give a colour of legitimacy to theft, murder and larceny – to propose, that is, a disguise for a situation ruled in fact by the principle that "might is right." Francis Jennings reminds his readers that Francisco de Vitoria "once remarked that an Indian 'discovery' of Spain would not have justified Indian sovereignty over Spain."[18]

That is an argument that bears on the one here, and could, finally, be a conclusion drawn from it, depending upon future historical developments we cannot now envisage. But the argument which embraces a recognition of the unbroken applicability of the *Royal Proclamation* to Canadian law, while in a sense a white man's argument, clears the way to a crystal clear recognition that white arrival and assumptions of power in Canada were and are firmly tied to powerful aboriginal rights that are currently almost completely transgressed.

> I will continue to dwell on the Bear Island matter in order to tease out continuing factors in the overall argument. They occur and reoccur in disputes across Canada in various forms. The Bear Island dispute is merely representative for the purpose of this essay. As I have said, the Temagamis never signed a treaty. That didn't prevent the Government of Ontario from stating it could deal with the Temagami lands as it wished. It was so adamant about its sovereignty over land that the federal government (with no evidence of any treaty, ever) began in the 1880s to pay some of the people annuities as if they belonged to another treaty that had been signed.

> It is important to observe that the Ontario government had long been conducting a process (policy?) to downgrade Indian entitlement in Ontario in a number of ways. The Bear Island dispute was only one of them.[19]

Ontario intransigence continued, and in 1970 it began to warn the Temagamis of Bear Island that they were trespassers on Ontario land and threatened them with prosecution for cutting firewood. The federal government took the line of least resistance in this difficult situation, bought the island from Ontario (which it did not own), and without a treaty set up unilaterally an official Indian Reserve in 1971. The federal government was honest enough to tell the Temagamis that, having taken the heat off their community, it would continue to press Ontario for a settlement of what was by then a very old treaty request. In fact, the federal legislation creating the Bear Island Reserve admits that the Indians had been "omitted" from the 1850 treaty that included some other Indians. In 1978, Ontario sued the Temagamis for a declaration of extinguished title, and the federal government not only reneged on its position that a treaty had been concluded but also abandoned the responsibility to them springing from the *Royal Pro-*

clamation of 1763. As well, in 1991, a decision of the
Supreme Court of Canada assumed that the Temagamis of
Bear Island had accepted the reserve there in 1971 as an
extinguishment of aboriginal rights. The problem of *tainted adjudicators* shows itself clearly.

But before that, the argument about whether the Temagamis had extinguished title was fought. Clark took the
case that was heard in Toronto in 1982-1983. In the pre-
trial hearings which are conventionally and by rule under-
taken by a judge who will not sit on the case – for reasons
of important niceties of fairness – the Chief Justice, for
some reason, declared that the pre-trial judge would also
take the trial. Formal applications to change that decision
were ignored. In the case, the Ontario government sued the
Indians for a declaration that their aboriginal rights were
extinguished and it asked the court for definition of unextinguished title. First extinguish title, and then say what it
is to have unextinguished title.

Much more could be said about the trial and the Bear
Island case. But it is sufficient for the argument here to say
that the courts would not allow the key point to be
addressed: had the Crown extinguished aboriginal title by
treaty and the process of treaty making which is law?

Now we must turn (or return) to those things which
reasonable and prudent people would expect of Canadian
law and due process. In the first place, why would the
Government of Ontario attempt to develop Temagami land
when no treaty ceding the land existed? Why would the
Government of Ontario threaten to prosecute the Temagamis for cutting wood and to remove them from Bear
Island? Why would the Government of Canada buy Bear
Island from the Government of Ontario when the
Government of Ontario could not prove title to it? Why,
subsequently, would the judge hearing the suit from the

Ontario government for a declaration that the Temagamis aboriginal rights had been extinguished refuse to admit the letter from the Minister of Indian Affairs assuring the Indians *after the creation in 1971 of the Bear Island Reserve* that aboriginal rights were still being negotiated? Why would the Government of Canada declare Bear Island an Indian reserve when the Temagamis were already living on it as unceded land? Why would the Chief Justice of the Ontario Supreme Court break a rule of practice and require the pre-trial judge also to be the trial judge when there was not a visible reason in the world why he should do that? Why would Revenue Canada fall upon Bruce Clark for tax arrears during the dispute and be willing to see his legal practice fail when there were ways in which it could have permitted him an extension of time under the circumstances?

The questions could go on and on. The ones above are representative. They are asked in order to make a point: very frequently in questions of aboriginal title and the powers of Native people, the actions of governments, courts and related institutions are deeply disquieting and give reasonable and prudent Canadians cause for alarm and for serious questioning. Many of them question, for instance, the disbarment of Bruce Clark from legal practice as not in any way proportionate to his behaviour.

What are the reasons for the aura of unease, dissatisfaction and disquiet surrounding legal arguments about aboriginal title and aboriginal powers? Perhaps Bruce Clark states the matter as simply as it can be stated: "Now," he writes, "in the end, it all seems so simple in terms of the principles ultimately involved. The natives were here first. The newcomers undertook legally to respect them and did not. And now the newcomers' courts are negating the rule of law by refusing publicly to address their ongoing role in the process."[20] That answer, of course, opens another key question: why are the courts negating the rule of law?

They are doing so for neo-liberal reasons. They are – whether consciously and unconsciously – sacrificing the terms of behaviour set up by a tradition of legislation, and they are doing so on behalf of the instruments of instantaneous gratification. They are involving themselves in the rejection of the *rule of law* historically enunciated, and they are doing so on behalf of the *rule of men* holding sufficient power to work their will. That is a very strong charge. But when one looks behind cases about aboriginal title, one frequently finds governments avaricious to increase revenue bases and corporations wanting access to unceded Native land for the purposes of exploitation. None of those parties has yet gone as far as to say that, if the people of Canada choose to have a referendum, they may erase "existing aboriginal and treaty rights." But they have been manipulating the devices of law in order to avoid having to face the fundamental questions that arise out of the *Royal Proclamation* of 1763. If they have not been manipulating the devices of law, why were there so many anomalies in the Bear Lake dispute? An approach respectful of the continuous fabric of law in Canada would admit the judicial errors of the past in relation to Native peoples. It would admit the governmental bulldozing of historical fact. It would probably grant third-party adjudication of the great wrongs in law against the Native peoples. I say "probably" because it is conceivable (though not probable in the short term) that the Native peoples and Canadian governments could so heal the rifts between them that they could sit together as equals and work through a respectful solution that would not, after all, wreck the country or deliver irreparable trauma to the non-Native population. With each passing day, however, the refusal to grant the reality of the continuous fabric not only causes continuing injustice to Native people, it taints the courts and it spreads the effects of injustice in an ever widening circle.

The continuing injustice to the Native people is immense. In his argument against the Ontario Law Society in relation to the move to disbar him, Bruce Clark refers to complicity in genocide. Specifically, he wrote of the Law Society's "abetting the crimes of treason and fraud and complicity in genocide, by turning a blind eye to the legal profession's role in the premature invasion of the unceded Indian territories, and the ensuing suppression of the natural, international and constitutional law which precludes the said invasion."[21] He has repeated, more or less, those charges before courts on a number of different levels. His claim of institutionalized genocide seems, to many, to be extravagant and unnecessary, even unfair. It causes alarm and anger among those to whom it is directed. But in the full recognition of his argument and the meaning of Indian title in the matter of unceded lands, the charge is not extravagant. For if the Native peoples had received justice on that matter, through Canadian history, there is every reason to believe the decimation of the population that has occurred (and is occurring) and the impoverishment of the people with all its consequent ills would not have come about. That is a heavy burden for Canadians to shoulder, and one that needs rectification without delay.

Clark's 1995 confrontation of Chief Justice Lamer of the Supreme Court of Canada would be funny in that regard if it were not so serious. Asked to consider whether the court had, in fact, jurisdiction in the matter of Indian land, the Chief Justice replied that he could not take up the matter within the case being heard; it had to be "started" in a lower court. Clark argued that it has been tried in eleven lower courts each of which said it was a matter of such weight that it had to be heard by the Supreme Court, and now the Supreme Court was refusing to hear it because it had not been raised in a lower court. Clark then added: "I wish to argue that the crime of genocide never occurs unless the court system of the country in which it is occurring is complicitous." And he told Chief Justice Lamer: "Your jurisdiction [is] as guardians of the sacred trust of civilization," to which Lamer replied: "Oh my God. I did not swear to that. I just swore to be a judge and try to do my best according to the rule of law." Clark pushed the idea by saying, "It fell upon you, whether or not you realized it. That it is the duty under which you labour." Chief Justice Lamer then rejected the idea in a strange way: "I must say, Mr. Clark, that in my twenty-six (26) years as a judge I have never heard anything so preposterous and presented in such an unkind way. To call judges of the Supreme Court of Canada and the nine hundred and seventy-five (1975) High Court judges of Canada accomplices is something preposterous. I do not accept that and I think you are a disgrace to the bar."[22]

Chief Justice Lamer's statement that he simply swore to be a judge and to try to do his best according to the rule of law seems humble and unpretentious, but it is also a cap on a judiciary which rejects the continuous fabric of law; one might say it is a way of refusing, in fact, the rule of law.

I wish to take the matter a step further. I say above that the continuing injustice to Native people taints the courts and spreads the effects of injustice in an ever-widening circle. I refer, finally, to what is called the Gustafsen Lake affair in British Columbia in 1995. Described in the briefest terms, Indians claimed a sacred ground on about eight hectares of a huge ranch. Ironically, the land was never ceded by the Indians in a treaty and so the very nature of ownership of the whole must be in question. A small group of Indians intended to hold a Sun Dance ceremony there, and a dispute erupted about the degree of Native ownership and their right to fence some of the land. The matter escalated in an alarming way. Armed white people arrived on the scene. Some Natives were armed. The RCMP became involved. They closed off a large area from anyone (press included) and delivered "reports" of events inside the area. Declaring the Natives a significant threat, the RCMP was "assisted" by the Canadian military in the form of military vehicles used in the dispute. Thousands of rounds of ammunition were fired by RCMP officers, and at least one land mine was used against the Natives there. Professor Tony Hall of the University of Lethbridge describes the response by the RCMP and supporting forces as "the biggest police and military operation in Western Canada since the military campaigns directed at Louis Riel and his Métis followers in 1885."[23] Trials ensued with convictions that have caused great division in opinion among Natives and other concerned citizens. Nothing good has come out of the Gustafsen Lake affair.

A part of the result involved spreading the effects of injustice in an ever widening circle and tainting not only the courts but institutions that stand in relation to them. During the "standoff," with a large area closed to anyone but RCMP, an officer contacted CBC on September 15, 1995, requesting air time to have a local Indian chief broadcast a special message into the Native camp. The request was said to be urgent, and the Director of Radio (DOR) in Vancouver was told by the RCMP officer that lives were at stake. CBC officials made a hasty decision and permitted the RCMP to have the chief make a broadcast. Subsequently, Tony Hall and John Shafer made complaints to the CBC ombudsman, David Bazay. He investigated and found the statements made by the RCMP officer about the situation at Gustafsen Lake were false.

Taking care to declare (for complex reasons) that his reply was not "a formal ombudsman's review," Mr. Bazay writes that the then-Managing Editor of CBC Radio News, Jeffrey Dvorkin, who authorized the broadcast, told Mr. Bazay "that this broadcast was a mistake, and that CBC's journalistic independence had been breached." The Managing Editor "says he received a telephone call from the then-Director of Radio in Vancouver informing him that the RCMP's Sgt. Montague had made an urgent request to broadcast a special message into the camp. His understanding was that a hostage taking was underway. The DOR in Vancouver was told by Sgt. Montague that lives were at stake and that only by broadcasting this special message would lives be saved. Sgt. Montague put a great deal of pressure on the DOR to comply. I [Jeffrey Dvorkin] had five minutes to make a decision about a situation I could not verify. I made the decision that CBC Vancouver could broadcast the special message believing the RCMP that lives were at stake. Mr. Dvorkin said this proved to be untrue, and he wrote a letter to the RCMP Commissioner to protest against the manner in which the CBC had been manipulated in order to help the police."[24]

At the trial of the Native defendants present at the Gustafsen Lake affair, police videos made of apparently private conversations were introduced. The films were often about strategy to be used at Gustafsen Lake and had been kept to be used for training purposes. Sergeant Denis Ryan, addressing the Police management Team in charge of the Gustafsen Lake affair, asks: "Is there anyone who can help us with our smear and disinformation campaign?" And he says: "Kill this [Bruce] Clark and smear the prick and everyone with him."[25] The films were shown at the trial. Large excerpts from them, including the above quotations, have been reproduced in a documentary film, *Above the Law. Part Two*, still available and shown to a large number of people in British Columbia and delivered to the press and broadcast media. No response has been heard from the RCMP Commissioner or other senior officers; no public investigation has been started; no senior people in the force seem to be concerned in even the slightest way. The extraordinary actions against Native people at Gustafsen Lake can only be described as alarming. Sgt. Montague's actions in relation to the CBC defy description. The fact that top RCMP officers, the Attorney General of British Columbia, and the courts did not move quickly to review publicly the acts and utterances of Sgt. Montague and Sgt. Ryan can only be described by using Chief Justice Lamer's word: the inaction is preposterous.

Clearly the refusal of Canadian governments and courts to uphold the rule of law as it applies to Native people in their rights to unceded land as proclaimed in 1763 is tainting the courts and spreading the effects of that injustice to an ever widening circle that is beginning to include the national media and the RCMP. Canadians may well ask where it will stop.

Legal professionals, academics and some others find themselves in a maze of argument about tenuous technicalities in aboriginal affairs. Bruce Clark erases the maze. Reasonable and prudent Canadians may be forgiven if they do not believe the courts are unable to address fundamental questions. And, of course, they are correct. Any government *could* start an action involving the questions with the express view of carrying it to the Supreme Court of Canada. The federal government itself has the power to refer questions to the Supreme Court, as it did regarding the legitimacy of a proposed federal, unilateral patriation of the constitution at the beginning of the 1980s. If the courts are not addressing the fundamental questions relating to unceded lands, they are responding to very powerful forces pressing upon them, the forces of neo-liberalism in Canada. To suggest the reasons are otherwise would compel inquirers to seek answers in the personal racism of judges and other distasteful individual motivations. Whatever their reasons, judges will not be able to hold out forever. The continuous legal fabric which Canada possesses is against them. The *Royal Proclamation* of 1763 is a vital part of Canadian law; its declarations as to the rights of Indians in relation to their unceded lands cannot be kept forever from full and fair examination by competent courts, wherever they can be found.

NOTES

I am indebted to Lyn Crompton, lawyer for traditional Native people and, now, graduate student in Law at the University of British Columbia, and to Professor Tony Hall, Native North American Studies, University of Lethbridge for rich discussion on the matter of this chapter. While they have made its strengths possible, responsibility for weaknesses rests with me alone.

1. Bruce A. Clark, *Indian Title in Canada* (Toronto: Carswell, 1987); *Native Liberty, Crown Sovereignty* (Montreal and Kingston: McGill-Queen's University Press, 1990); *Justice in Paradise* (Montreal and Kingston: McGill-Queen's University Press, 1999).
2. Brian Slattery, "Understanding Aboriginal Rights," *The Canadian Bar Review*, Vol. 66 (1987), pp. 727-783.
3. Peter Kulchyski, "Introduction," *Unjust Relations: Aboriginal Rights in Canadian Courts* (Toronto: Oxford University Press, 1994), p. 6.
4. That is said in full consciousness that legal professionals in Canada (and elsewhere) make much of the fact that U.S. judicial statements declare the rights of Indians in unsurrendered lands *before* the War for Independence and settle on principles established by the Imperial government. No one, unfortunately, has compared dates of "Indian Wars" and agendas of state genocide with the declarations of judges in courts. Bruce Clark makes the point in *Justice in Paradise* at p. 46 that when, in 1832, Chief Justice Marshall confirmed Native sovereign jurisdiction, President Andrew Jackson is reputed to have said: "Chief Justice Marshall has made his decision; now let him enforce it." Clark goes on to make my point: "Thus Jackson in effect declared an illegal and unjust war on the native nations."
5. *Royal Proclamation*, October 7, 1763 (excerpt), in Derek G. Smith, ed., *Canadian Indians and the Law: Selected Documents 1663-1972* (Toronto: McClelland and Stewart, 1975) pp. 2-3.
6. Nancy Brown Foulds, "The Quebec Act," *The Canadian Encyclopedia* (Edmonton: Hurtig, 1985) p. 1524.
7. Fred Anderson, *Crucible of War* (London: Faber and Faber, 2000).
8. Michael Rose, "Roar of American Independence," *Guardian Weekly*, Vol. 163, No. 23 (30 November-6 December, 2000), p. 15.

9. Clark, *Indian Title in Canada*, p. 1.

10. Clark, *Justice in Paradise*, p. 12.

11. Clark, *Native Liberty, Crown Sovereignty*, pp. 84-123.

12. Quoted in Clark, *Indian Title in Canada*, p. 11.

13. Clark, *Native Liberty, Crown Sovereignty*, p. 39.

14. *Ibid.*, p. 41.

15. *Ibid.*, footnote # 96.

16. Clark, *Indian Title in Canada*, p. 99.

17. *Royal Proclamation*, in Smith, *op. cit.*, p. 2.

18. Francis Jennings, *The Ambiguous Iroquois Empire* (New York: W. W. Norton, 1984), p. 4.

19. Claudia Notzke, *Aboriginal Peoples and Natural Resources in Canada* (Toronto: Captus Press, 1994), pp. 67-73.

20. Clark, *Justice in Paradise*, p. 40.

21. *Ibid.*, p. 246.

22. *Ibid.*, p. 242.

23. Tony Hall, *Evidence Presented To Address Canada's Request To Extradite Mr. James Pitawanakwat from the United States for His Involvement in the Gustafsen Lake Standoff in British Columbia in 1995 at the Request of Mr. Paul Papak, Assistant Federal Public Defender in Portland, Oregon, September, 2000*, p. 9 (unpublished).

24. David Bazay to Professor Anthony Hall, 24 November, 1999 (unpublished).

25. Clark, *Justice in Paradise*, p. 243-244.

CARGO CULTS AND CORPORATE CULTURE

HOWARD A. DOUGHTY

Millenarian cults arise under conditions of social stress when traditional belief systems no longer adequately explain social upheavals, natural disasters or other extraordinary challenges to normal life. Common to the ideologies of cults is the necessity of accommodating conflicting values, reconciling contradictory perceptions, and incorporating abrupt material transformations into a coherent *Weltanschauung*, often under conditions of social oppression – real or imagined. Each cult seeks to combine elements of the past with visions of the future in a dramatic synthesis – a "myth-dream" – that will exorcise former and current injustices and evils, provide a strategy for practical action, and initiate a time of civil peace, economic prosperity and spiritual salvation. The cargo cults of Melanesia were the products of encounters with people – mainly of European ancestry – who exploited the indigenous peoples but who possessed material goods that the natives coveted. The combination of traditionalism (often in the form of anticipated aid from the ancestors), a vision of a future attack upon and expulsion of some or all of the aliens, and a promise of the consequent reward of unrestricted access to foreign material goods (cargo) were the three major elements of the cults' mythologies. Usually under the leadership of a charismatic prophet, cargo cults arose suddenly and often were as quickly repressed, or else collapsed when the promised utopia failed to materialize. Moreover, just as the accountants, customer service representatives, product designers, receptionists and webmasters of Fortune 500 companies would not readily recognize themselves as members of twenty-first century "cults," so it is expected that the Melanesians to be discussed here had no such self-image. They merely understood their destiny in a particular way and were prepared to act upon that understanding.

Millenarianism

Older than *Exodus* and as potent as the *Gospels*, millenarianism can be as dangerous to social élites as the revolutionary eschatology that emerged in Europe in the late Middle Ages, as astonishing as the religious virtuosos among revolutionary flagellants, as potentially egalitarian as the sixteenth century English Ranters, and as "obsessed by the apocalyptic phantasm and as filled with the conviction of its own infallibility" as to constitute "a true prototype of a modern totalitarian party."[1] According to anthropologist Lucy Mair, "the essence of the "cargo cult" is the belief that when the millennium comes the ancestors will bring with them vast quantities of the imported goods to which all Europeans appear to have unlimited access, while they are out of the reach of native cash incomes."[2] Thereafter, there would be abundance, tranquility and a welcome absence of outsiders.

Millenarianism is to be distinguished from utopianism. Both speak of a future idyllic world but, unlike utopianism, which depends mainly upon human agency, millenarianism stresses supernatural intervention in bringing about a reconstruction of the world. Indeed, as Roger Emerson has pointed out, "the biblical tradition has consistently worked against utopianism while furthering chiliastic and millenarian beliefs; it has done so because the transformations of man's life which are revealed are really the works of God and not men."[3]

Modernity, however, has produced a variety of millenarian and quasi-millenarian movements that depart significantly from earlier religious models. Ernest Tuveson, for instance, presents examples of two contrasting prophets who were contemporaries, Mary Baker Eddy (1821-1910) and Karl Marx (1818-1883). Eddy expressed confidence that the great hope of salvation was soon to become fact; Marx, too, was convinced of the impending collapse of capitalism and the evolution of democratic socialism. There can be no doubt that religious faith was central to Eddy's Christian Science doctrine but, Tuveson says, "the resemblances of the Marxist pattern of history to millennial ideas are too striking to be entirely coincidental."[4] Accordingly, the several Judeo-Christian-Islamic variations of the YHWH cult offer up an impressive inventory of chiliastic fantasies and orgies of religious violence that are replicated in some forms of political revolution. In powerful secular analogs to religion, historical determinism is substituted for the divine will.[5]

Included in the religious catalogue are the portentous visions in Chapter 7 of *The Book of Daniel*, the apocalypses of Ezra and Baruch in the first century AD, the slaughter of European Jews in the Second Crusade (1145-1153), the career of the twelfth century prophet Tanchelm, the alleged divinity of thirteenth century Emperor Frederick II, the brief and bloody histories of heretical sects including Taborites, Hussites, the followers of Thomas Münster and John of Leyden, plus dozens of others who proclaimed that they were living in the "Last Days," that the "Second

Coming of the Messiah" was imminent, and that the way must be prepared for the "Final Judgement" by putting all unbelievers – Jews, Muslims, and Christians of other than the "true faith" – to death by fire and sword. Recent manifestations of the phenomenon in the suppression of women and religious freedom by the Taliban in Afghanistan and by associated acts of international terror and retribution are also transparent.

The devotion of the faithful to such madness is common in religious societies; interpreting secular variants, however, requires some (but not much) elasticity. As Albert Camus pointed out half a century ago, history – the enthusiasms of such divinely inspired grotesques as Islamicist ideologues notwithstanding – has largely replaced god as the inspiration for eschatological atrocities, of which the twentieth century certainly had more than its share.[6] Although their victims may be forgiven for indifference to the distinctions between, for example, Nazism and Stalinism, we should nevertheless understand that there are material particularities to be discerned among various forms of secular tyranny. Openness to diversity in the conceptual grounding of social dementia appears to be the trend among experts in the history of ideas. Openness is fitting, as well, in the study of the enormous variety of social movements that meet the essential criteria of millenarianism. Some are more or less irrational than others; some are more or less dangerous.

The Cargo Cults of Melanesia

My first exposure to Melanesian cargo cults came in the form of a black and white documentary film that dated from the early 1950s. My clearest recollection of the film is a scene in which about a dozen New Guinea natives stood in a jungle clearing that they had made into a crude "runway" to which they expected to lure an airplane carrying cargo. As extra enticement, the aboriginals had fashioned a simulated aircraft, a skeleton really, made of tree branches, vines and bits of cloth. The scene impressed me as merely bathetic. It gave no hint of the depth and diversity of the cults nor of their similarity to other millenarian movements across space and over time. The natives that were filmed seemed dull and dispirited, almost as though they had reluctantly been flown in from Central Casting in Port Moresby and were going through the motions of being naïve primitives for the entertainment of even more naïve anthropologists carrying on the tradition of Margaret Mead.[7] Who knows? Perhaps, they were.

Only in the late 1960s did I become aware of the archetypal power and tremendous variety of cargo cults. Their diversity is nicely captured in the juxtaposition of two representative examples described by anthropologist Marvin Harris.

One of the earliest recorded cargo cults arose in 1893 at Milne Bay in New Guinea. There, reports Harris:

> a prophet foretold volcanic eruptions and tidal waves followed by the appearance of the ancestors' ship and a period of great abundance of pigs and fruit and all good things. In order for this to happen, however, all the available pigs and other foodstuffs had to be consumed and all European goods had to be abandoned. After the tidal wave failed to appear, the colonial officials jailed the prophet to prevent further disturbances.[8]

Then, in 1914 on the island of Sabai in the Torres Strait which separates Australia from Papua-New Guinea:

> Prophets promised the arrival of the ancestors in a steamship laden with money, flour, canned goods, and other valuables. With the aid of the ancestors, the British administrators would

be killed or driven off the island, and there would be a period of great abundance. The leaders of the movement, inspired by Wesleyan missionaries and impressed by the enmity between the Germans and the British, called themselves *German Weslin*. The colonial administrators intervened, exiled the leaders, and prohibited further cult activity.[9]

The energy of the cults can be grasped both politically and psychologically. The first example is irrational and mystical; the second is sophisticated and political. Both, however, give an important role to the ancestors, outline definite actions to be taken, and promise serenity and material abundance in the future. The former relies upon a supernaturally induced *tsunami*; the second depends on military arms and imagines at least a temporary alliance with the Germans against the British, a strategy of "divide and conquer" in reverse. In later cults, sacrificial and the expiatory destruction of existing material goods and the call for the expulsion of outsiders would recur, as would ambiguous relationships with outside cultures that might be asked to furnish chimerical external allies, arms and ideas. A few more examples should make plain some common characteristics of the cargo cults.

One was led by the prophet Evara, who foretold a steamship bringing flour, rice, tobacco and rifles. F. E. Williams' account reads as follows:

As of 1919, the Elema of coastal New Guinea had experienced waves of European influence: missionary teachings, early experience as plantation laborers, introduction of the few items of European hardware the Elema could afford. In that year, a movement broke out among the Elema that for a time set whole villages into "head-he-go-round," a psychological state reminiscent of the Dancing Mania of plague-ridden medieval Europe. People lost control of their limbs, reeled drunkenly and eventually lost consciousness. Who formulated the ideology is not clear. Central in it was a belief that the dead would return, bringing with them a fabulous cargo of European material goods – knives, cloth, canned goods, axes, and so on. Within a year, most overt forms of the movement had subsided.[10]

Another cult briefly won followers shortly after World War II. It involved Malaitan Islanders, who had participated in the volunteer Melanesian Labor Corps with U.S. soldiers in the Solomon Islands. Having had experience with British colonials that sharply contrasted with their encounters with the better-equipped and more egalitarian Americans, they sought to unify the Melanesian peoples under the leadership of nine tribal chieftains. The chiefs were to negotiate with the returning British for the establishment of a communal society based roughly on military lines. Under their proposed "Rule of Brotherhood," a system formulated largely by a Malaitan Islander named Nori, the Solomon Islanders were to be united in a "social, economic and political millennium when they would be free and wealthy like the Americans."[11] Political action including strikes and demonstrations failed to win British sympathy, and the leaders were promptly jailed. Supernatural doctrines of the millennium and faith in the impending return of the friendly Americans failed to sustain the movement and, by the early 1950s, it had died out.

Finally, on the New Hebrides island of Espiritu Santo, cargo cults had been known for decades. In 1923, the prophet Ronovuro predicted that the Europeans would prevent a cargo ship from landing. Accordingly, a plantation owner was killed as a warning to other Europeans not to interfere. The ship did not arrive; but government officials did with predictable results. It was one of the few uprisings that resulted in a loss of life. Nonetheless, in 1939, this time under the direction of the prophet Tsek, the cult re-emerged.[12] For over half a century, cargo cults failed and, where they were perceived as sufficiently disruptive and dangerous, they were promptly suppressed.

From Tragedy to Farce

After World War II, the mysterious departure of the Americans precipitated formidable cults. Many of the more unusual cargo cult practices involved those same Americans. On the island of Tanna (sometimes spelled Tana) in what is now the Republic of Vanuatu, also in the New Hebrides, the John Frum (sometimes spelled Frumm) cult flourished in the 1940s. Built upon traditions of polygyny, dancing and drinking – all supposedly suppressed by missionaries – this anti-European movement cherished an old GI jacket (the tattered remnant remains on display today) which was once worn by John Frum(m), who was held to be "King of America" and deliverer of the anticipated cargo. The Frum cult persists and every February 15th "John Frum Day" is celebrated to the apparent delight of tourists (it is given full attention in local travel guides and international vacation brochures).[13] It features "a military parade where the male tribesmen, bare to the waist and with the letters 'U.S.A.' painted on their backs, march under the orders of two elders dressed as U.S. Army sergeants." It also emphasizes the Red Cross, both as an enduring symbol of Frum and, perhaps, a clue about his original identity. (This assumes, of course, that he actually existed and was not, as some insist, either "John *from* America" or a pidgin rendering of "John Brown," the would-be liberator of American slaves who would return to liberate the Melanesians). Participants, of course, remain sincere. Following Moses Maimonides, who remained convinced that the Messiah would come though "he may tarry," one chief said in a 1970 interview, "people have waited nearly 2,000 years for Christ to return, so we can wait a while longer for John Frum."[14]

Stranger still was the Lyndon Johnson cult. The prophet Bos Malik organized it in 1964 on the island of New Hanover in the Bismarck Archipelago. He demanded that the Australian government permit the islanders to vote for U.S. President Johnson in their village elections as a way to influence him to deliver cargo. Then, instead of paying Australian taxes, Malik insisted that the money be paid to him so that he could "buy" Lyndon Johnson, entice him to reveal the secret of cargo, and reap the rewards for all. According to Marvin Harris, "Malik prophesied that the liner *Queen Mary* would soon arrive bearing cargo and U.S. troops to liberate the islanders from their Australian oppressors."[15] When these events failed to occur, Malik accused the Australians of stealing the cargo. The tax revolt continued to spread. By 1965, more than $82,000 had been collected to "buy" LBJ and more than 150 cultists were in jail.

Americans have, of course, not always fared as well in cargo cult history. On islands captured by the Japanese during World War II, downed U.S. airmen were regularly turned over to the enemy by natives who had been assured that cargo was coming but that it had been delayed by the hostilities. A speedy victory for Japan, they were assured, would thus hasten the delivery of the treasured goods.[16]

Religion, Technology and Magic

The cargo cults, according to Peter Worsley, can best be interpreted as religious movements "in which there is an expectation of, and preparation for, the coming of a period of supernatural bliss."[17] Worsley and others find the explanation for the cults in the pattern of colonial oppression. Their analysis emphasizes asymmetrical power relationships between cultures and derives an interpretation of cults as attempts – albeit ineffective ones – to overcome this situation. Alternatively, some offer the theory of relative deprivation especially among natives whose expectations of access to Western products had once risen but were subsequently lowered, as a more powerful explanatory device.[18] Whether one prefers the former political or the latter psychological explanation, it is at least clear that cargo cults present a problem of strategic cultural interpretation. Marvin Harris declared:

> The confusion of the Melanesian revitalization prophets, is a confusion about the workings of cultural systems. They do not understand how the productive and distributive functions of modern industrial society are organized. To them the material abundance of the industrial nations and the penury of others constitutes an irrational flaw, a massive contradiction in the structure of the world. I find it difficult to disagree with them.[19]

The existence of confusion can itself be stressful and it is one function of social myths to reduce such stress by incorporating contradictory, inexplicable or cosmically unfair data into a satisfactory system of explanation and legitimation. Such systems are often built upon appeals to magic. "Preliterate people are not necessarily prelogical," observed Ralph V. Barrett; thus, "knowledge related to practical work activities such as canoe building or fishing was clearly separated from magical rituals which attempted to deal with dangerous, uncertain conditions not easily controlled by the actions of human beings. Poor work habits were distinguished from poor magic."[20] Practical knowledge is necessary to the survival of a culture, but sometimes magic is added to deal with imponderables. So, Malinowski wrote that "magic, as the belief that by spell and rite results can be obtained, enters as a complimentary factor."[21] Lagoon fishing relies almost solely on human effort and invention while open-sea fishing requires "magical ritual to secure safety and good results."[22] Coping with the related puzzles of external political domination and astonishing material innovations certainly made magical interventions appealing to twentieth-century Melanesians. They certainly underscore the perception that desire for cargo did not imply a general conversion to western ways of thinking. As Umberto Eco suggests, "when the first European ships appeared on the horizon, bringing with them unknown goods, the natives thought that one day deities would disembark from them to bring them happiness. That to my mind is a typical millenarian attitude. The cargo-cult myth doesn't indicate that Melanesian and Polynesian populations began to believe in a version of history considered as constant progress."[23]

Even in times of relative social stability, myths have their place. They work to account for the world and define humanity's place in it. Religious mythologies of origins and endings, sin and redemption, and the relationships among humans, gods and nature are non-rational ways of contending with the contingency of human existence and reconciling mortality with consciousness, especially consciousness of mortality. Enduring myths can be passed on over generations in an oral tradition or codified, pressed into doctrine and transmitted as organized religious texts. Social myths work in rather the same way, with the main difference being the myths' main themes. Thus, various secular notions of "human nature" will be deemed "common sense" and will incorporate views about humanity's allegedly inherent dispositions on such controversial topics as cooperation vs. competition, personal liberty vs. social obligation, procedural fairness vs. traditional privilege and so on, according to the social needs of the time. They will, in short, define a culture.

When, however, stable social patterns are irrevocably disrupted and continuity is destroyed, when irreconcilable contradictions appear and the world is "turned upside down," myths function to attempt a reintegration of social life and understanding. This is the circumstance that led Weber to his analysis of charisma, and it is the charismatic myth and the myth-dream of trial and salvation that are at issue here. Charismatic leaders and charismatic myths are necessarily temporary and, at their best, facilitate a transition to new, just and harmonious social arrangements. Their content may vary wildly and quite different myths may follow one another in rapid succession. They nonetheless share the aim of easing transformation and bringing a happier order out of unpleasant chaos. In times when people are disoriented and traditional beliefs are shaken, potent new myths can sometimes accommodate new realities, manage cultural contradictions and reconcile ideological inconsistencies. As Burridge says: "The discrepancies of detail are matched by the congruence of ends."[24] Like other combinations of exceptional ideas and practices that are reactions to staggering social change, however, cargo cults are inherently unstable: "merely temporary; they break out like a rash, and die away."[25]

There are typically three phases in the natural history of a cargo cult. First, there is the "creation of a myth-dream."[26] Second, there is the attempt "to realize the myth-dream."[27] Third, there is the "aftermath," a time to resolve the problem of "promises not made good," when "the dramatic fervor of a cult cannot long be sustained."[28]

Marvin Harris tells us that it would be easy to dismiss cargo cults as ephemeral products of primitive minds. The prophets could be seen either as scoundrels who prey upon the innocence of their followers or as delusional psychopaths. Cult behaviour could be interpreted as "autohypnosis and mass hysteria if there were nothing mysterious about how industrial wealth gets manufactured and distributed." In fact, however, he insists that "there really is a cargo mystery and the natives are justified in trying to solve it."[29] The mystery exists in a similar way and to a similar extent for North Americans too.

Currently, advanced technological societies are experiencing unsettling political and economic changes that have been likened to those accompanying the industrial revolution. These changes threaten the sense of progressive continuity that has largely defined modern civilization for over two centuries. They are now undermining what both the employees of global corporations and the general public have understood as common sense. To interpret these changes and our responses to them, we could do worse than to reflect upon the experience of others who have also undergone impressive alterations in their lives. Here, then, is an opportunity to relate the experiences and responses of remote Melanesian tribes to contemporary North America and to tease out the ideological and practical similarities. Some aspects will appear as analogous, others as oppositive. Relationships, however, will be unmistakable.

Corporate Myth-Dreams

The task of the cargo cult was to explain social turmoil, call upon magical traditions for help, and inspire action to reclaim control over social, political and economic arrangements by ridding the community of aliens and alien culture. It was to achieve these ends while simultaneously ensuring that the material benefits of modernity would not only be retained but would be equitably distributed among the people after the Europeans were expelled. The task of the corporate myth-dream is to explain social turmoil, call upon ideological traditions for help, and inspire action to reclaim control over social, political and economic arrangements by ridding the community of unproductive people and obsolete practices. It was to achieve these ends while simultaneously ensuring that the material promises of globalization would provide abundance that will be fairly distributed (i.e., allocated according to individual market value) among the people after the enemies within had been exorcised.[30]

North American society is currently experiencing a rapid change in the capitalist mode of production. IT (Information Technology), global markets, international finance, the dismantling of social programs, the replacement of the public sphere by private interests and the decline of national sovereignty as a result of various free trade agreements have already had profound effects upon personal lives, social values and cultural understanding. There is fear that continued change and its personal, social and cultural consequences will be devastating. The plans for a new round of "oil wars" only complicates and compounds concerns about electoral legitimacy, corporate crime, plutocratic power and ecological degradation. The underlying anxiety remains. Some are poised to believe Kurt Vonnegut's prediction of the fate of the U.S.A.:

> We will be a Third World country. The only consolation is that every other country will be Third World too. (You watch!) Thanks to the inevitable aftereffects of imperialism, of taking people's land away and busting up their cultures, this will be a Third World planet.[31]

To deal with the stress resulting from the difficulty of reconciling established values, dissonant perceptions of the meaning of change and revolutionary technological innovations, major political and economic institutions have wrapped themselves in the neo-liberal myth-dream.[32] It is a capacious worldview that seeks to meld elements of the past (personal responsibility, family values, individual competition) with intimations of the future (high technology, borderless states, unrestricted markets) in a mighty synthesis that will exorcise foreign and domestic demons (the "evil ones" and their multicultural dupes), extirpate former and current injustices (moral permissiveness, identity politics and public debt) and initiate a time of personal integrity, moral rectitude and economic prosperity as defined and determined by the ancestral spirit of the free market's "invisible hand." Democracy (especially in its robust and egalitarian, participatory form) is seldom mentioned. Popular judgements are restricted to outcries *against* specific evils such as child pornography, public support of the arts, legal principles that emphasize the rights of accused criminals and lax toilet training, and calls *for* tougher immigration laws, welfare restrictions, school vouchers and capital punishment.

Neo-liberalism is, at base, the ideological expression of the wish to restructure international capitalism in the interest of global firms. In it, liberty is distinguished from life and the pursuit of happiness and affirmed to the exclusion of equality and fraternity. It is not "all citizens" or even "all men" who are given the primary benefit of "natural rights"; through privatization of the public sector and deregulation of the private sector, what is emancipated above all else is capital.

Like cargo cults, neo-liberalism will metamorphose in response to particular crises, but it will collapse, if at all, only when the promised utopia fails to materialize and when something approaching Marx's anticipated immiseration of the proletariat (this time on an international scale and with the added complication of environmental spoliation) promotes radical political consciousness.[33] In 1952, Kurt Vonnegut sketched out a pessimistic local scenario for such a development in his first novel.[34] Using a fictionalized General Electric as a microcosm, he provided a model dystopia in terms of the social implications of high technology in late capitalism. Immiseration was less economic than psychological as redundant workers were denied even the dignity of useful drones; as with cargo cults, a revolutionary uprising, based on the native American ghost dance, was futile.[35] By 1972, he expressed the view that neo-liberalism implied more than existential angst and an opportunity for suicidal revolt against the malaise of modernity. It also promised limitless and grisly technologies of death. Vonnegut carved this inscription on a tombstone for humanity in an excellent essay about the Republican Convention in Miami: "The winners are at war with the losers, the prospects for peace are awful."[36]

In proposing neo-liberalism as an analog to the myth-dreams of Melanesian cargo cults, I begin with the commonplace assertion that in human affairs no ideology, no cult, nor much of anything else arises *ex nihilo*. Each time a millenarian movement asserts itself, it does so in a context of social and intellectual turbulence. For any number of reasons dominant social ideas, whether described as religion, science, philosophy or folklore, can be brought into disrepute. When that happens, one of the principal functions of a cult and its charismatic leadership is to offer a positive alternative to the moral confusion that results when traditional beliefs are undermined.

Modern economic life is in just such a state of confusion. The current cultural context must therefore be described, and the depth of the disrepute into which some of the more libertarian aspects of the so-called "folklore of capitalism" have fallen, must be identified.[37] There has long been plenty of dubious capitalist folklore about. Talk about capitalism and capitalist relations of production has gone on for centuries. It has accompanied the several transformations in material production and distribution that have carried us from the decline and fall of feudalism to the rise of mercantilism, through the industrial revolution and, now, into the post-industrial era. Each of these major changes has required an equally significant adjustment in the stories people tell themselves about what the economy is, how it works, and how it ought to work.

The stories that have been most popular and that have acquired the status of hegemonic myths are familiar enough. From classical economists to Keynesians, from Calvinists to social Darwinists, from Thomas Jefferson's paean to independent farmers to the curves and arrows of Paul Samuelson's outrageously fortunate Nobel Prize-winning economics textbook, theorists, ideologues and popularizers have hawked notions that, each in its own way, gave the establishment's preferred account of who was getting what, why and how. Each one was also able to persuade people that there *was* something called "the economy" and that it could heat up, cool down, get sick, recover, and get moving again. Like Phil Ochs' madonnas, bulls and bears could "dance the minuet for naked millionaires."[38] This reified economy, which exists quite apart from the actual activities of real women and men, is crucial as the focus for a myth-dream. It is an abstraction that carries more intellectual weight than the work and worries of flesh-and-blood people in real-life circumstances.[39] What is more, the economy is populated by protagonists that are among the most peculiar personae in the human drama.

Almost three-quarters of a century ago, Gardiner Means and Adolph Berle presented the then-novel thesis that free enterprise, based on unhindered competitive individualism, had already been displaced by the emergence of the modern corporation as a bizarre legal entity.[40] Virtual before virtuality, corporations are created in law by governments as "artificial persons," and are "treated like any other independent person with its rights and liabilities appropriate to itself."[41] But, of course, corporations are not individual persons. They are associations of shareholders who, unlike whole persons or even business partnerships, enjoy a special status. They are protected by the principle of limited liability. They are dissociated from the management of the enterprise. They have no obligation of loyalty to the enterprise. They are unique in that they finesse even the inconvenience of death, since corporations continue in perpetuity regardless of the demise of any of their particular shareholders. Corporations are unnatural. They are aberrant legal fictions. According to Gregory Bateson, they are "self-maximizing entities which are precisely *not* persons and are not even aggregates of whole persons. They are aggregates of *parts* of persons."[42] Richard Gwyn, a political columnist and former aide to ex-Québec Revenue Minister and ex-Canadian Communications Minister and Postmaster-General Eric Kierans, points out that in creating the corporation governments made:

> an immortal thing unlike individual entrepreneurs – capable of limitless growth, virtually unchecked by shareholders or government. It was a new entity, unaccountable and untouchable, vulnerable only if it failed to earn profits, a task easily accomplished by the devices of oligopoly and quasi-monopoly. Add globalism, and you can jump to today in a single leap.[43]

This wisdom is received, albeit grudgingly, by academicians

and best-selling mystery novelists alike. Sometimes they write grumpy briefs on political economy which attempt to find historical precedents for current processes. So, as early as 1970, economist Kari Levitt wrote about "the new mercantilism"[44] and, more recently, novelist Scott Turow sought a medieval metaphorical link to globalism. So, Turow's hard-bitten anti-hero, Mack Malloy muses:

> Somebody ought to sit down and think about this, because your corporate types are soon going to be a stateless superclass. It's the Middle Ages all over again, these little unaffiliated duchies and fiefdoms, flying their own flags and ready to take in any vassal who will pledge his life to the manor. Everybody patting himself on the back because the Reds went in the dumper is going to be wondering who won when Coca-Cola applies for a seat in the UN.[45]

Outbreaks of worker discontent and fitful protests against the World Bank, the World Trade Organization (WTO), the International Monetary Fund (IMF), various "free trade" agreements, individual human rights abuses, sporadic genocides, Gulf wars, and ecological disaster notwithstanding, capitalists in most societies have spun triumphant stories about themselves. They have dissuaded the bulk of the population from contemplating, much less attempting, anything close to revolutionary *praxis*. Whether bought off by incremental reforms and marginal wage increases, struck down by staggering police power, mesmerized by CNN wargasms, or persuaded that anything more than polite attempts to win mild material improvements would be futile, most people at most times and in most places accept the ruling élite's version of reality. From time to time, however, the establishment falters. Sometimes it even seems to lose control, or to be caught either in such shameful falsehoods or monstrous contradictions that its legitimacy is questioned.[46] Opportunities then exist for charismatic leaders with alternative myths and dreams.[47]

Capitalism's Nightmares

In the age of literacy, the oral tradition of charismatic leaders from Moses onward has been transformed. Tales of antique heroics and impassioned public displays of rhetorical skill helped make and maintain ancient Greek democrats, Roman Senators, traditional North American Indian leaders, occasional Nazis, Sir Winston Churchill, evangelical Christians and Fidel Castro. Today, we disdain, as demagogues, politicians who cannot reduce their messages to a 10-second sound bite or a bullet on a web site. Mass politics has been tamed in liberal democracies. Public opinion, anonymously manipulated by the media and massaged by the custodial state, "does not tyrannize," wrote Tocqueville, "it hinders, compromises, enervates, extinguishes, dazes, and finally reduces each nation to being nothing more than a herd of timid animals of which the government is the shepherd."[48] Absent vigorous and informed public debate, politics becomes lowbrow entertainment with elections in a contest with "reality" television and disclosing only which leadership show has produced the biggest box office receipts for its corporate investors.

Now, however, opposition to entrenched power has come to depend on rhetorical skills transferred to the printed page, on conspiracies and guerrilla bands, or on both. Sometimes tactical advantage has been gained by provoking nervous politicians and plutocrats to overreact in ways that undermined rather than enhanced their authority. The gambit can be deadly. From the mythical General Ned

Ludd and his Army of Redressers risking the gibbet to Chartists and Communists demanding a free press and the right to vote, from George Washington winning his revolution as much through Edmund Burke's speeches at Westminster as on the battlefields of America to Castro winning his revolution as much through Herbert Matthews' articles in the *New York Times* as in the *sierras* of Cuba, the story has been the same. Especially in the "developing" worlds (Europe in the nineteenth century, elsewhere today), opposition movements must either establish their own exceptional regimes or they must fail and join the measureless heap of martyrs rotting in the rat-infested composter of history. In time, however, even diffuse, anonymous and defeated peasant and worker uprisings have fertilized larger organizations. Led or inspired by Fourier, Saint-Simon, Proudhon, Bakunin, Kropotkin and Marx (in their anarchist, syndicalist, socialist or communist variants), they created a patchwork quilt rebuttal to bourgeois ideology, the revolutionary myth-dream.

The revolutionaries of the industrial era never fully realized their myth-dreams, but they *did* win the bourgeois right to vote and a relatively free press. In doing so, they, too, frequently drew upon traditional community values while simultaneously directing their anger toward the new industrialists and the alien machinery that they employed. They, too, thirsted for an equitable distribution of the material abundance brought about by technological innovation, a fair share of the "cargo" their own toil had produced. They, too, were brought down in Haymarket, Homestead, Pullman and Ludlow, and in Estevan and Winnipeg. They occupied mines and auto plants and, in time, they lived *The Life of Riley* and bought their beer in *Archie Bunker's Place*. The broad similarities in the circumstances faced by industrial workers at the beginning of the nineteenth century, Melanesians entering the twentieth century from the lifeworld of preliterate tribalism, and postmodern Wal-Mart shoppers being greeted in the foyer of the twentieth century, need little elaboration.

Whereas, however, the nineteenth and early twentieth centuries generated revolutionary myth-dreams to counter the claims of bourgeois ideology, today it is the mythology of corporate culture, not that of the workers, which seems, paradoxically, more comparable to that of the cargo cults. Corporate cultists, of course, dispute neither the claims nor the rhetoric of established power and authority; on the contrary, they desperately embrace it. They own PCs. They watch DVDs. They drive SUVs. They are proud of the corporate logos on their leisure wear as they cheerfully convert themselves into sandwich boards for the fashion industry. They must be actively convinced to hate themselves as a prelude to expiation, but I am getting ahead of myself.

Let us first understand that, throughout modernity, economic folklore has emphasized the progressive rationalism of both the oppressed and the oppressors. On the moderate left, there was Tommy Douglas seeking to build out of medicare and old age pensions "a new Jerusalem" for Canadians.[49] On the right there was Walt Disney importing the man who gave London the buzz bomb in World War II to give *Tomorrowland* Sunday evening substance equal to Ronald Reagan's Sunday night promise that "at General Electric, progress is our most important product."[50] The past centuries have seen the effulgence and eclipse of any number of temporarily dominant ideologies and have witnessed the inchoate reply of any number of defiant myth-dreams. Thus, in the 1960s, posters of Dr. Ernesto Guevara found their way into teenagers' romper rooms, where middle class rebels sang along with the young Bobby Dylan and Joan Baez and Janis Joplin and

Gracie Slick, and channeled into the Woodstock Nation. While reading sermons by Regis Debray, student radicals may have mixed rum with cola. Meanwhile, Coca-Cola, anticipating the global economy, produced the honeyed hymn line "We'd like to teach the world to sing in perfect harmony"[51]; and Pepsi-Cola authorized young people to be part of the "Pepsi generation," to read *Playboy*, and to rise to the ecstasy of "feelin' free, feelin' free." Pepsi was also connected to the overthrow and assassination of Chile's President Salvadore Allende through its associated company Frito-Lay's links to *El Mercurio*, Santiago's most despicably reactionary daily newspaper.[52] So it went.

The justificatory rhetoric of the ruling élite has been sustained by more than catchy commercial jingles, intertwined directorships and interlocking dictatorships. A sequence of deeper belief structures has acquired the status of conventional wisdom and has also been supported by whatever passed for social and sometimes even natural science at the time of their popularity (Didn't we once believe in IQ tests? Aren't we still searching for a "crime gene"? Don't we sometimes imagine that the Human Genome Project will yield evidence that poverty is heritable?).[53] So, it is convenient to date the intellectual origin of the coherent expression of core capitalist beliefs from the late eigthteenth and early nineteenth century classical economists, especially the cherished Adam Smith, alleged mentor to the "Frito Bandito."[54]

The collapse of feudalism, the rise of new factors of production, the triumph of the profit motive and the dominance of the market mechanism all helped vindicate and explicate new forms of wealth based initially on trade and later on manufacturing, but no longer on agricultural land (at least not land in Europe). Initially, the industrial myth-dream of relentless material progress, scientific advance and technological ingenuity was, together with its social and political implications, neither unambiguously accepted nor endorsed. That Edmund Burke, the purported father of modern conservatism, was skeptical is no surprise:

> But now all is to be changed. All the pleasing illusions that made power gentle, and obedience liberal, which harmonized the different shades of life are to be dissolved by this new empire of light and reason. All the decent drapery of life is to be rudely torn off. All the super-added ideas, which the heart owns, and the understanding ratifies, as necessary to cover the defects of our weak and shivering nature, and to raise it to a dignity in our own estimation, are to be exploded as a ridiculous, absurd and antiquated fashion.[55]

That Karl Marx should speak with just a slight whiff of what others might mistake for nostalgia is notable:

> Constant revolutionizing of production, uninterrupted disturbance of all social relations, everlasting uncertainty and agitation, distinguish the bourgeois epoch from all earlier ones. All fixed, fast-frozen relationships, with their train of venerable ideas and opinions are swept away, all new-formed ones become obsolete before they can ossify. All that is solid melts into air, all that is holy is profaned. The bourgeoisie has stripped of its halo every occupation hitherto honored and looked up to with reverent awe. The bourgeoisie has torn away from the family its sentimental veil, and turned the family relation into a pure money relation in the place of exploitation veiled by religious and political illusions, it has put open, shameless, direct, naked exploitation.[56]

The Theory of Scientific Management

Such tumult certainly required myth-dreams of celebration, of mourning, and of rejection. Dark satanic mills, child labour, and unprecedented pauperism were the price of progress, the inspiration for romantic lamentations and the impulse for political rebellion. Fate, however, decreed that celebration would ultimately prevail. So, the theory of scientific management is among the firm bases of neo-liberalism.

Special attention was paid to the oversight of the industrial labour process from the outset of the modern economy. The *Enclosure Acts*, dating from the late sixteenth century and ongoing, drove peasants into cities. Then, cottage industries were, from the late eighteenth century, forcibly integrated into large factories and eventually into the assembly line system of manufacturing. So, rigid control of work and workers in these new circumstances was crucial to social order and economic success. Reviewing the history of professional management through the more recent stages of capitalism, Bennis and Mische tell us that the managerial practices of "the majority of organizations today are the product of several centuries of economic expansion, free-market evolution, and industrial engineering. All these practices," they add, "have evolved from concepts first proposed by such management luminaries as Frederick Taylor and Abraham Maslow."[57]

Such stars inhabit a constellation that is passing strange. Taylor's story of scientific management which made deskilling, routinization, employee monitoring, rigid factory discipline, and workplace alienation into a twentieth century art form and Maslow's fable of a hierarchy of human needs culminating in the apex of self-actualization could hardly appear more at odds. One accentuated efficiency at the expense of the human worker; the other made the humane treatment of the worker the key to efficiency. Yet, each tale was told in corporate boardrooms and each had a profound effect on management practice. As well, each had in common the core concept of efficiency. In repetitive industrial processes of the kind that is increasingly being turned over to machines, the self-worth of the individual factory hand was of little interest to the owner; making maximum use of muscle power while awaiting automation was the chief concern. As the preponderance of paid work shifted from farms to factories, Taylor's methods came to dominate [58]; then, as manufacturing gave way to service industries, Maslow became fashionable. Still, as Harry Braverman reminded us: "if Taylorism does not exist as a separate school today, that is because, apart from the bad odor of the name, it is no longer the property of a faction, since its fundamental teachings have become the bedrock of all work design." According to Braverman, "Taylorism dominates the world of production; the practitioners of 'human relations' and 'industrial psychology' are the maintenance crew for the human machinery."[59] For a time, the professionalism and quasi-professionalism of the white-collar worker in the service sector implied that mental labour was more meaningful than manual labour and more deserving of the care, attention and coddling of human resources experts. Now, however, that both manual and mental labour are seen to be more and more removed from physical production, a new story is needed. It must be able to reconcile at least a minimum of human dignity and at least modest economic expectations with a society in which regular employment is expected to be a privilege and a career a luxury.

The contributions of contemporary social scientists to the neo-liberal myth-dream continue to be momentous. Academic management theory and its penetration into corporate culture reflect the relationship among ownership, management, profit and ideology. Indeed, some form of ideology has been required to justify privilege and explain poverty ever since the beginnings of a social division of labour. Religion served well for a long time and is not to be discounted even today. The transition from the rational, progressive and secular industrial economy to the intellectual, social and economic instability of postmodernism has, however, displayed an extraordinary number of mental twists as we negotiate the bridge to the postpresent. Particularly revealing are the intellectual machinations of the contemporary psychological priesthood.

Among human studies, psychology has been most adept at winning promotion to the status of a "science" (though economics, the most successfully quantitative of the social studies, runs it a very close second). Psychology has also most unambiguously declared itself on the side of power in the necessary conflicts between employers and employees.[60] The specialty of "organizational psychology" is an excellent illustration. Almost every standard text in the field takes pains to stress methods of motivating workers to higher productivity, teaching managers "leadership skills," and increasing "teamwork."[61] Almost none address issues of union organization (except to disclose tactics to combat it), collective bargaining rights and the maintenance of worker solidarity in the face of managerial intimidation. Instead, psychologists and others happily participate in the "visioning" and dissemination of myth-dreams that do for business what cargo cults did for Melanesians. They would rectify past wrongs, expiate guilt, identify an enemy and use magical, mystical chants – combined with stalwart actions – to redeem the traditional values of capitalism in new and confusing times. Like the cargo cults, most of the myth-dreams of late capitalism have a shelf life only a little longer than that of a genetically modified muffin. Myth-dreams come and go in rapid succession for the simple reasons that they do not work. People tire of hearing about their failures and, of course, memory has to be cleared to open space for new entrepreneurial soothsayers, seers and prophets of profit to rush in and grab the mantle of fleeting business fashion. Moreover, given the bias against remembering history (or what happened last week), this is no serious shortcoming. Examples of corporate myth-dreams turn up and turn over with Roto-rooter frequency.[62]

Building on Taylorism 1: The Japanese Miracle

First, it was only a few years ago that organizational theorists were all agog about Japan.[63] In North America, popular culture in the 1970s began with Altamont and Kent State; they ended with the Bee Gees and Theory Z. Before Michael Crichton and Sean Connery treated us to the novel-cum-cinematic xenophobia of *Rising Sun*, William S. Ouchi had successfully worked his Hegelian magic on organization theory. Out of the static polarity of the carrot (Theory X) and the stick (Theory Y) approaches to management, he synthesized Theory Z.[64] It was, he claimed, the key to beating the then-successful Japanese at their own game. The marvelous accomplishments of Japanese firms reconstructed as extended families came as no surprise to some U.S. companies such as IBM, from which the Japanese borrowed many of their organizational reforms. Still, North Americans were skeptical of an organizational model that seemed ill suited to the culture of competitive individualism. Even the disconcerting fact that Japan's industrial success was derived from U.S. corporate innovations was acceptably finessed by theorists. They opined that the Japanese had copied a U.S. template (often said to be IBM) and applied it to their own culture and circumstances, which were more conducive to the repression of personal ambition and the celebration of collective achievement.[65]

What few chose to notice at the height of the Japanese

hype was that millions of Japanese jobs were, in today's jar-
gon, "outsourced" to contract employees whose cottage
industrial mode of production generated neither decent
wages nor comprehensive benefits. Being a lifelong
employee of a major corporation was certainly worthwhile,
but it was a privilege that many had to forego. In retro-
spect, it is "outsourcing," not the sense of corporate community, that may be the real legacy of the Japanese miracle.
Nonetheless, the core content of the Japanese corporate
myth-dream was that, by guaranteeing lifetime employment, encouraging non-specialized career paths, promoting
decision making by consensus, insisting on collective
responsibility, introducing informal methods of control,
keeping income disparity between senior management and
workers within sane limits, and embracing the joys of
karaoke, employee morale would bloom like a chrysanthe-
mum. Efficiency would rise. Profits would swell. Mouthing
the mantra, *kaizen*, employers and employees would
"grow" mutual respect to the benefit of all.

Building on Taylorism 2: Democracy & Flexibility

Second, beginning with the truism that change was afoot in
the land, other analysts sought related solutions to the
problem of how to make rigid, stuffy, hierarchical bureau-
cracies less . . . well, bureaucratic. "Just-in-time" to facilitate corporate reengineering and in a rather more compas-
sionate incarnation than was to appear a couple of decades
later, who else but Warren Bennis would appear and would
join with sometime counter-cultural favourite Philip E.
Slater to succor the spirit of empathy and celebrate the
virtues of personal growth? Disdaining "a model of power
based on coercion and threat," Bennis endorsed a "new
concept of organizational values, based on humanistic-

democratic ideals, which replaces the depersonalized mechanistic values of bureaucracy."[66]

To be fair, Bennis admitted even then that the future might not be unambiguously euphoric: "Coping with rapid change, living with temporary work systems, developing meaningful relations and then breaking them all augur social strains and psychological tensions."[67] Still, he forecast no worse than a "nation of itinerants, moving continually on an irregular and perhaps even non-recurrent circuit of jobs." Unwilling to dwell on the prospect that the next temporary job might be the last, Slater added: "What is mildly characteristic of the academic world and the large corporation today will become accelerated throughout the economy."[68] Recalling the happy wanderings of vagabond scholars and superannuated graduate students in the late 1960s, as well as Professor Harold Hill clones leading big parades of employee motivators, innovation facilitators, communication enhancers and change champions down the human resources superhighway all the way to River City, worse fates could and should have been imagined.

Building on Taylorism 3: Empowerment & Innovation

Other engaging ideas took their allotted times. Participative management was promoted. Job enrichment was encouraged. QWL (Quality of Working Life), TQM (Total Quality Management), and BPR (Business Process Reengineering) became the sequential acronyms of choice. Transactional analysis for managers was marketed. Everyone obsessed on "excellence." The underlying factor in all of these myth-dreams was, of course, the same as what had underlain Frederick Taylor's restructuring of the workplace and had thoroughly dehumanized work (despite his oft-quoted and hideously hypocritical assertion that his first principle was and always would be "the welfare of the working man"[69]). Whether brutally authoritarian or warmly humane, the bottom line was invariably the bottom line. As its sponsors noted on the 50th Anniversary of the Hawthorne Studies: "What impressed management most were the stores of latent energy and productive cooperation that could be obtained from people working under the right conditions."[70]

In North America, popular culture in the 1980s – the decade of *Wall Street* and *American Psycho* – began with Ronald Reagan and Margaret Thatcher and pretty much ended with Ronald Reagan and Margaret Thatcher, along with the inevitable results of their tenures.[71] In the case of the U.S.A., this meant the quadrupling of the national debt, the Savings and Loan debacle, the Iran-Contra debacle, the Canada-US Free Trade Agreement, the killing of Muammar Qaddafi's two-year-old daughter, the proud military victories over Grenada and Panama, and the kidnapping of President Manuel Noriega. Less was being said about the humane treatment of workers and much less was being done. In Ontario, the Ministry of Labour's Quality of Working Life Centre was closing its doors; OD (Organizational Development) was replacing QWL. The language of externally imposed organizational crisis was superseding the language of internally generated organizational health. Indeed, the holistic model of the firm as an organism, which theoretically blended the health of the individual employee with that of the organization, was being jettisoned. Performance standards, efficiency measurements and individual appraisals made it clear that (especially non-union) workers were again alone and vulnerable.

Building on Taylorism 4: Union Bashing

As previously mentioned, few school texts, fewer trade publications in organizational behaviour, and no self-promotional CEO autobiographies speak well of trade unions. Except for the occasional mention of the possibility of co-opting union leaders or undermining certification drives, unions are either ignored or scapegoated. John L. Mariotti, for instance, spent slightly more than a page of his book, *The Power of Partnerships*, urging that companies "partner" with collective bargaining agents.[72] Distressed by the inefficiencies forced upon free capital by organized labour, James Martin lamented "work rules and job restrictions. An electrician," he cried, "could not saw wood; a carpenter could not change a light bulb." This "appalling" situation, he claimed, "imposed by unions" was at best anachronistic and at worst destructive of a productive economy.[73] Rare is the mildly magnanimous approach of Warren Bennis, who scolded U.S. leaders including "the country's top CEO, Ronald Reagan, [who] expressed the basic animosity that too many CEOs feel toward both unions and workers when he fired the air traffic controllers. Our lives," he wrote, "are literally in their hands, but the president nonetheless saw them as expendable and got rid of them, because they dared to ask for salaries that were commensurate with their responsibilities. As the president went," he continued, "so went corporate America. We have entered into a period of union bashing that is unprecedented in modern times."[74]

Meantime, the eerie unworldliness of most alleged experts was heavily underscored in the conclusion to a popular college psychology text of the time. Discussing "future issues in organizational behaviour," its author lists the importance of "inflation," of "employee rights and organizational ethics," and the prediction that "unions will gradually show a greater interest in the findings of behavioral science research."[75] Inflation is mainly an economic concern of the rich and has, in any case, been under control for some time. Employee rights remain relentlessly under attack while organizational ethics remain free to find their market value. As for trade union interest in behavioural research on promoting productivity, it remains understandably small. Organizational psychology, however, has continued to supply management with a stream of data and analysis about working people. As Martin Nicolaus once observed, "the corporate rulers of this society would not be spending as much money as they do for knowledge, if knowledge did not confer power."[76]

At the spiritual centre of the contemporary corporate myth-dream is the concept of globalization.[77] Organizational theorists like Bennis have come near the mark when they have predicted that the emerging global economy will produce social disruption. The future of workers and of work itself is endangered. Here is one typical prophecy:

> Global markets will become saturated, technological advances will be short-lived, growth in disposable incomes will be slow, income gaps will widen and the workforce will be transitory. Employment practices are changing from lifetime careers to transitory arrangements with contract personnel. Organizations will have a smaller percentage of full-time employees with core competencies and a larger percentage of highly specialized contract workers.[78]

Globalization and the New World Corporation

These trends have taken on the metaphysical quality of inevitability not only among corporate executives and government planners but also within the general public. The magic formula is recited throughout the mass media, in management seminars and on the shop floor: "Since we don't operate in a vacuum," say the corporate coaches, "it's important to examine some of the key trends in our environment. These are conditions and forces having a big effect on us now, and which we expect to be even more influential in the years to come."[79] It is seldom mentioned that these key trends are not written in the stars. They are not supernaturally enforced. They are not iron laws of history. They are the sum of decisions made for transparent political and economic reasons by actual human decision makers who could choose to do otherwise.

It is assumed here that those in charge of major corporations and financial institutions know very well what is happening around them and what the implications are for the rest of us. It follows that the myth-dreams of corporate ideologues are intended mainly for middle managers, those below them on the company ladder, the mass media, and eventually the general public. They create an artificial ideological context in which the inevitability of massive "dislocations" can be explained, made acceptable and combined with a promise of renewal. The three devastating Ds of public policy – downsizing the public sector, deregulating the private sector and devolving responsibility for social programs to the weakest and poorest levels of government – are only part of the many-faceted neo-liberal myth-dream.

In addition, authors like Martin are quick to acknowledge that "the new-world corporation says to its employees: Promotion prospects are low. We cannot guarantee regular salary raises. And there is no job security. The age of entitlement is over."[80] He is, however, clever enough to suggest that this "bad news must be counterbalanced with a new deal that is attractive to employees: 'This is an excit-

ing place to work . . . You own your own employability.
You are responsible. If you make yourself valuable, you will
be employable.'"[81] If, however, you merely do your job
well and do not put in unpaid overtime creating imaginative new hoops through which to jump, you are finished.

In such stressful circumstances, if those who are vulnerable are not distraught, they may at least be distracted.
There is therefore a need for a myth-dream that will legitimate an artificial Hobbesian world, a myth-dream that will
encourage a war of all against all. For a very long time
racism, sexism, xenophobia and religious intolerance
worked relatively well to ensure that people scrapped over
table scraps. The heightened tensions and trepidations occa-
sioned by globalization demand more.

The importance of competition and the aims of business are sometimes couched in the language of ecstasy:
"Satisfied customers don't count these days. If you want a
booming business you have to create Raving Fans."[82] More
common is the term "delight," a state of mind perhaps a
step or two removed from delirium but certainly more
effusive than standard business expectations in steadier
times. "Head-he-go-round" enthusiasms make for changes
that "are a revolution in the nature of the enterprise. This
revolution is characterized by massive automation, fluid
organizational structures, and a new human-technology
partnership. When it runs its course in society," Martin
rhapsodizes, "this transition will be much larger than the
Industrial Revolution."[83]

Creating Crises

Successful corporate manipulation of the cult of change
depends upon the creation of a crisis or at least the perception of a crisis. According to one survey, "competitive

pressures" were identified by 64% of respondents as "the event or compelling factor that triggered," in the material instance, a BPR effort.[84]

The alleged need for change is always said to be externally imposed rather than initiated from within the organization, much less from within the imagination of a shrewd CEO. Hence, the role that the prophet played in the cargo cult is now performed by very senior management – duly assisted by postmodern clones of Uriah Heep – who must "recognize and articulate an 'extremely compelling' need to change." According to Carr and Johansson, "the compelling need is driven by the marketplace and the competitive environment," just as cargo cults are brought into existence by the intrusion of a powerful alien culture that simultaneously stimulates a desire for the aliens' material wealth.[85]

Preparatory work for extensive crisis creation dates from the 1960s when philosophers concerned with the study of ethics induced a major mutation in education. Encouraged by popular volumes such as *Situation Ethics*, they successfully insinuated into the curricula of schools, colleges and universities a consideration of moral questions that was detached from venerable concepts of right and wrong, to say nothing of the religious notion of sin.[86] Often this transformation was presented as an exercise in "values clarification." This process effectively cut ethical decisions off from traditional beliefs and located them, instead, in the domain of personal preferences and individual interests. Sin was replaced by solipsism. Indeed, the very change in language from morals to ethics to mere "values" – the ideas, actions or things to which any specific person may or may not attach "value" – particularized and thereby trivialized the discussion of right and wrong. Instead of considering actions (now called "behaviours") in terms of eternal verities and universal principles, ethics was recast as rational decision making on an economistic cost-benefit model. The primacy of self-interest was rarely more clearly adumbrated than in the "learning activity" known as "lifeboat ethics."[87] This experiment in ethical thinking – imagining oneself in an overcrowded lifeboat with few rations and a stormy sea – assumed a hostile environment, scarce resources, overpopulation, untrammeled competition and the implied threat of violence. Students were asked to take this Hobbesian-cum-Malthusian model seriously as a miniature of existing society and work out ethical principles appropriate to the situation. If some chose to jump overboard, it would be unsurprising to learn that they did so not with the selfless intent of saving others but in the desperate attempt to escape nihilism. Corporate culture raised (or lowered) this philosophical simulation game to the next level. Borrowing from the language of deep-sea oil rigs, it invited us to contemplate strategies for innovation premised on the assumptions of the "burning platform." Given the choice between death by fire if we stay and death by water if we jump, we are asked to think up strategies for the survival not of a few souls in a boat, but an entire floating organization. The corporate version employs similar assumptions and compels contemplation of analogous actions but its implications are more general and it insists that, whatever happens, our traditions – normal life on the rig – are to be permanently sunk.

Being thus conditioned, we may now understand why failure to achieve a suitable climate of crisis is the first and major deficiency of would-be corporate prophets in the real world. The "failure to drive people out of their comfort zones" causes over 50% of companies to fail to change even before they have started the process of visioning (hallucinating). "Error #1," says John P. Kotter, Konosuke

Matsushita Professor of Leadership at the Harvard Business School, "is not establishing a great enough sense of urgency."[88]

Companies that triumphantly embrace change are said to do so through the actions of what seems on the surface to be an oxymoron, an organizational charismatic leader. With respect to charisma, Max Weber taught us to think of it as arising in a situation of authentic crisis when a spontaneous leader wins authority through the power of personality. He also taught that such leadership is necessarily fleeting for it must either lead a return to tradition or else be routinized through bureaucratization. What many of us did not expect was that leaders would be encouraged to create their own crises, their own charismatic situations.[89] Had we paid more attention to his passionate remarks at the close of *The Protestant Ethic and the Spirit of Capitalism*, we might not have been so surprised. In 1904, Weber saw the beginning of the twentieth and foresaw the beginning of the twenty-first century, at least in the U.S.A. He spoke then of living now in an "iron cage" in which "the pursuit of wealth, stripped of its religious and ethical meaning [becomes] associated with purely mundane passions, which often actually give it the character of sport."[90] Let the games begin.

Corporate Charisma

The great global game needs strong leadership to convince people that they are indeed standing on a burning platform and that survival depends on the "organized abandonment" and "systematic innovation."[91] Dead workers walking . . . Societies that have become used to progress, to generational increases in the material standard of living, to some social entitlements as in the U.S.A. and to such added benefits as universal, publicly supported postsecondary education and a publicly funded health care system as in Canada, are to be mesmerized by a magnificently crafted myth-dream if they are to be convinced of the inevitability of a disastrous decline in their quality of life. They must be preternaturally guided to a belief in their own political enfeeblement and the unreasonableness of their longstanding hopes and expectations. The future is fated, and folk must insensibly submit to the spells of men like economist Ian Angell of the London School of Economics who unabashedly tells us that "it's not just that we can't change things, *but we can't even think about the possibility of changing things; to do so is old-style thinking.*"[92]

To persuade Canadians, for example, that Canada cannot afford a medicare system that costs less than 10% of the Gross Domestic Product and must, therefore, accept a US-style two-tiered system that costs Americans about 15% of their GDP, requires more than the usual political sleight-of-hand. It takes men with the self-confidence of Milton Friedman and his soothing, scientific-sounding chants about the non-accelerating rate of unemployment (solving unemployment by driving down wages) to avoid "sounding mean-spirited and callous, as well as moralistic" while "providing justification for government inaction on the job front – a key element in the cult of impotence."[93] It requires immense popular faith in the trance-talk of our economic superiors when they tell us what we can and cannot afford, when they denounce the sin of profligate spending, and when they scourge us for living so long beyond our means. We are asked to imitate Canada's gift to *Saturday Night Live* Mike Myers and his metal head buddy Dana Carvey as they brayed before the seductively outstretched Madonna – "We are not worthy!"

This process of growing self-loathing takes, according

to the late political columnist and former Progressive Conservative party strategist Dalton Camp, a belief in "the psychic powers of free markets and free trade, and the divine inspiration of the profit motive" to inspire a brilliantly choreographed "celebration of the decline of human civility [and] corporate proprietorship of the political process enforced by the economic dogmas propounded by a corporate owned monopolistic media."[94] It takes a population that has allowed itself to be gulled by politicians, policy experts and such neo-liberal pundits as Terence Corcoran, Andrew Coyne, and David Frum into putting their faith in global competition and entrepreneurship.[95] To walk as zombies into the future we must first, it is plain, kill our pigs. Meanwhile, at the level of individual organizations, mini-magicians cast spells of restructuring, reengineering and retreat in the sure and certain knowledge that their vision is not only the most cogent one but, for the time being, the only one. Debate is unnecessary. Debate is futile. Debate is impossible. Wrote management consultant Douglas K. Smith: "If you are a leader, you *will* personalize your vision of how people can get through a period of behavior-driven change. Your actions will put a subjective stamp on the organization's future. There is no escaping that."[96] There is, it seems, no escaping much of anything.

Corporate Rhetoric

In the magical words of global transformation, dramatic imagery abounds; however, even in the enchanted discussion of "key" environmental trends, the urgency of contemplated change is sometimes most effectively expressed in folksy language. So in 1988, Michael Hammer won the rapt attention of high executives with his admonition to combine the benefits of IT and TQM by stating: "It is time to stop paving over cow paths. Instead of embedding out-dated processes in silicon and software, we should obliter-ate them and start over."[97] Equally bluntly, Peter F. Drucker declared: *"The first policy – and the foundation for all the others – is to abandon yesterday."*[98] The dead pigs and mango pits of New Guinea surely have their func-tional equivalents in ideologically obsolete and ritually abandoned business practices. The current cycle of corpo-rate myth-dreams has other notable parallels with ineffec-tual Melanesian mind-sets, large among them being the capacity for rhetorical flourishes.

Melanesian prophets won over disciples by means of their oratorical prowess. Corporate ideologues are masters of pithy prose and, today, succinct sound bites. Their writ-ten commentaries fill single pages. Their paragraphs are set off by bullets. Their slug lines started on 25 May, 1916, when the *Chicago Tribune* printed Henry Ford's timeless insight: "History is more or less bunk." Having passed the 85th anniversary of that priceless slice of sagacity, it is plain that commercial, industrial and financial neophiliacs and those who are swept up in their orgy of reinvention have largely been won over by Ford's substance and style. Moreover, it is not only history that has been dropped from corporate discourse but the moral restraints of phi-losophy, aesthetics and organized religion as well. Previous blue bloods, we should recall, felt the need to justify their wealth by pointing out how well they met their social obli-gations by displaying good taste in the funding of art gal-leries, museums, universities, libraries and other worthy public monuments to their own tax deductible generosity. Dedication to the higher achievements of civilization and well-publicized obeisance to the Church combined to give at least the illusion that something more than avarice encouraged the rich in their pursuit of riches. If greed was a sin, then philanthropy was a pleasing penance. Of course, some sensible people recognized that the piety of the affluent was self-congratulatory and politically motivated hypocrisy. For them, Nicholas Von Hoffman's collection of the aphorisms of the arrogantly rich was more revealing. "The public be damned," was an utterance of William H. Vanderbilt. "I have always had one rule. When a workman sticks up his head, hit it," was attributed to Carnegie executive Henry C. Frick. And who could outdo Malcolm Forbes' classic "He who dies with the most toys wins"?[99]

Once, it is true, old-fashioned capitalist ideology was more artlessly propagated than it is today. Young people actually read inspirational Horatio Alger stories. As a child in grade five, I remember being compelled to read a tale featuring no less a tycoon than John D. Rockefeller. As I recall it now (about fifty years later), the story described a confrontation between the oil magnate and a humble worker. The worker had the cheek and impertinence to criticize Rockefeller for having so much while others had so little. For his pains, he was treated to a lecture in which the millionaire explained how his fortune was invested in industries that performed the socially useful tasks of providing goods for the marketplace and jobs so that people would have the money to buy them. Capitalism was thus "spun" as an especially worthy form of philanthropy. The leveling instinct of the poor worker, who had stupidly suggested that Rockefeller share his wealth, was shown up as socially useless. Rockefeller concluded his argument by saying that he could indeed give away his fortune in equal parts to all and, in that case, he concluded: "Here is your portion, eleven cents!" In that way I was inoculated against the foolishness of socialism, whether expressed in the Sermon on the Mount or the propaganda of the Co-operative Commonwealth Federation, soon to become the

New Democratic Party. Now, however, that history is said to have ended, no cover story is needed; wealth is allowed to be its own reward.[100]

As *Harper's* editor, postmodern Jeremiah and Brian Mulroney in-law, Lewis Lapham said: "There is no market for ideas in the United States. There is a market for slogans. There is a market for acronyms."[101] So the myth-dream of the WTO and the IMF can be dreamt in the minimalist style and those declared surplus to requirements can be shrugged off with the comment: "Let them eat ideology."[102]

Corporate Rulers

A second area for comparison is the universal capitalist advantage, the means by which our rulers rule. Melanesians could not figure out why the alien rulers held sway. For them, power always embodied some moral element. Success meant good magic; failure implied the enmity of the gods. Although not always transparent, the will of the spirits was always in play. For this reason, imperial power was doubly difficult to decipher. Not only was its moral or spiritual component obscure, but it was also hegemonic. No ordinary magic could stop it. No spirit could modify it. It bordered on the omnipotent and defied attempts at mollification or negotiation. Nothing less than a millenarian myth-dream would suffice to bring the power of the outsiders down.

North Americans experience the capitalist economy as similarly dominant. "Capitalism," avers Lester C. Thurlow, "has a current advantage in that, with the death of communism and socialism, it has no plausible competitor."[103] It is teleologically unchallenged. What escapes such dehydrated analysis is the fact that pure capitalism, understood as the combination of the lawful exchange of goods, free enterprise, and competitive individualism, has never existed, does not exist, and never will exist. First, illegal activities (anything from tax avoidance by small contractors who give reduced rates to cash-paying customers to international drug cartels) are common business practices. Second, the language of *laissez-faire* economics is little more than a smoke screen for oligopolistic control of the production and sale of goods and services. Third, within firms, anything other than mindless adherence to the company line is deemed treason. As corporate apologist James Martin put it: "corporate politics are a menace – the only enemy should be the competition."[104] Of course, even Martin's proposition is incredibly naïve. The work of former Canadian prime minister Mulroney is more revealing. His brokering of the infamous deal to extricate agricultural giant Archer Daniels Midland from a messy multimillion dollar lawsuit and criminal charges against its leaders for market manipulation in cahoots with their global "competitors" is more to the point. That point was made in the process of sorting out matters of anti-trust violations and international price-fixing when taped FBI evidence captured this exquisite sentence uttered by a Japanese executive to his ADM competitors: "The competition is not the enemy, the customer is the enemy."[105] None of this denies capitalist advantage; it merely says that capitalism is not what capitalists say it is.

Corporate Ritual

Ritual is a third important ingredient. Melanesians employed rituals internally to bolster morale, encourage enthusiasm and convey information about what was to be done. Similar practices in corporations, including fascinating ceremonials such as the development and celebration of mission statements, easily match the most solemn invocations of the spirits of tribal ancestors. Conformity once enforced by dress codes (white shirts only) and the compulsory singing of the company song at the beginning of IBM office hours are now amusingly antique. For outrageous "head-he-go-round" shenanigans, however, nothing beats corporate group humiliations masquerading as motivational sessions and bumptious exercises in company boosterism bordering on Nuremberg rallies. *"Ein volk, ein reich, ein Führer"* may be a trifle excessive as a symbol for describing what happens when ardent cultists from Amway to Mary Kay get together, but only a trifle. Such group therapy does for employees what Parris Island did for U.S. teenagers on their way to Vietnam. Such is the stuff of corporate indoctrination. Most ritual behaviour, however, is displayed in relations with the media in the form of press releases, press conferences and press interviews that are mediated through both print and broadcast media to the public.

Often, these rituals come into play at moments when the future of the myth-dream seems uncertain. This is done to ensure that even instances of failure or near-failure do not seem to compromise essential corporate principles. Whereas cargo cults *never* got cargo, in a climate of aggressive corporate expansionism, well-publicized problems are made to seem the rule-proving exception. In November 1999, for example, CEO John Roth could boast that "the market capitalization of Nortel Networks is now greater than the market cap of Ford Motor Company." Investors were buying Nortel stock at about $40 per share. The bubble was blowing up. Roth saw Nortel's future as "exploding." By August, 2000, Nortel stock was valued at over $120 a share. In October, it sank to $80 but Roth predicted over 30% growth in the following year. In February, 2001, the stock was at $30 per share and Roth reassured investors that he was achieving his goals for the company. By June, less than two years after hitting its peak, Nortel was selling at pennies over $15, a drop of about 87%. Nortel had a Canadian record $19.2 billion quarterly loss. It had put 30,000 people out of work in six months. Still, Roth remained "focused on getting the pain over with." His cheering section, including Prime Minister Jean Chrétien, insisted "Nortel is a very good company, a very strong company," and Industry Minister Brian Tobin added "There's no doubt in my mind they'll get through this. Nortel will continue to be a Canadian champion."[106] Despite an ecstatic overbuilding of the IT industry, a global glut in fibre optic and Internet equipment, and Nortel's aggressive corporate acquisition program, the myth-dreamers remained until their promises imploded; but, unlike US banks, they were not too big to fail.

On 16 January, 2001, in another widely publicized business story, CanWest Global's President and CEO, Leonard Asper treated the Canadian Club in Winnipeg to this slightly delirious tribute to the "convergence" of media corporations: "In the future, journalists will wake up, write a story for the Web, write a column, take their cameras, cover an event and do a report for TV and file a video clip for the Web. What we have really acquired is a quantum leap in the product we offer advertisers and a massive, creative, content-generation machine." With increasing concentration of ownership of TV stations and newspapers, the future of serious journalism, diversity of opinion and an informed citizenry grows dim. Meanwhile, under Asper's charismatic leadership, *The National Post* was "down-sized," the venerable Canadian magazine, *Saturday Night,* was jettisoned (rising only briefly under new own-

ership), and CanWest Global's corporate over-reach landed
it in financial troubles and ignominious bankruptcy protection.

For the best in media hyperactivity, however, the press
conference on a grand scale is the international summit.
High order politicians and bureaucrats have typically used
these events as functional equivalents of Royal Visits in the
days before the reconstruction of the House of Windsor as
the consummate dysfunctional welfare family.

Entering talks with their final press releases already
prepared, the participants' main goal has been to reassure
skeptical publics that their leaders are, indeed, addressing
important issues such as environmental protection and universal human rights. This charade has, however, been dam-
aged by such events as the refusal of signatory nations to
live up to the minimal ecological objectives identified in
Rio de Janeiro and by the failure of any number of UN
International Years to demonstrably enhance the lives of
women, children and other living things. So leaders have
tried to shift their attention to the safer ground of international trade. Photo-ops, however, have been less charming
after the "battle in Seattle," the "pepper spray summit" in
Vancouver and the June, 2001 shootings in Stockholm. So,
as Tony Blair stridently defended the rights of protesters to
protest but not to engage in "undemocratic anarchy" of the
sort that made it necessary for the police to use bullets on
them, it seems time to reconsider. Like the real economic
summits held by real corporate decision makers, they may
have to be conducted secretly, or at least in remote mountain resorts. But, of course, unseen public displays of
authority are oxymoronic. What use is a ritual if no one
sees it? What good is an execution if it is only viewed on
closed-circuit television? Myth-dreamers certainly have
some serious tactical thinking to do. Fortunately for them,

the "war on terrorism" has given some breathing room; still, social, political and economic issues will not be set aside forever.

Corporate Rationalization

Finally, there is the incantation of rationalization. Melanesian prophets sought to integrate past, present and future in a seamless myth-dream uniting the mystical with the pragmatic, the spiritual with the technological. For corporations, this integration takes the form of frequent announcements of corporate mergers, articulation agreements, vertical integration and horizontal expansion indicating that bigger is not just better but is essential for survival. The devotion to quantitative methods to yield longitudinal analyses of a firm's performance (bean counting with a buzz) represents just one step down the road to collaboration, consolidation, collusion and, perhaps, the formal combination of labour and management. The bottom line has always been foremost in the thoughts of corporate leaders; however, it is evident today that it is becoming the exclusive thought. Some pockets of resistance remain. Small bookstores, hardware stores, and convenience stores plead their cases as "big boxes" swallow them up. Quaint main street shops beg for government assistance in the struggle against suburban malls. Even comics such as David Letterman and Jay Leno – at some $20 million a year – whine engagingly about the "suits" and their calculated indifference to artistic integrity. Like the King's old foole, corporate jesters enjoy some license. They excoriate senior executives in amusing late-night monologues performed for the profits of intricately integrated publishing-television-music-film-internet conglomerates.[108] Capital concentration moves relentlessly on.

The interim stage of the consolidation process is typified by joint ventures among "friendly rivals." In the automobile industry, for example, it is no longer easy to determine which vehicles are manufactured in North America, Asia or Europe simply by noting the brand name. An automobile bearing a traditional North American "Big Three" name might well be partly a Japanese product and *vice versa*. This is fashionably known as the synergy of shared production.[107] One result is fuel for passionate U.S. free trade critics from Pat Buchanan to Ralph Nader and similarly for organizations such as the Council of Canadians. Another is the realization that cultural factors are being obliterated as standardized criteria of performance measurement are imposed from Los Angeles to Toronto, from London to Tokyo, from Singapore to Seoul, from Milan eventually to Moscow. The next stage – already well underway in some industries – is the formal merger. As the Daimler-Chrysler deal has demonstrated, the road to internationalization can be bumpy.[108] Cultural differences have not yet been entirely eliminated. Still, the preferred end of the myth-dream is clear. It is the truncation of the nation-state and the triumph of the virtual manufacturer.[109] It is the replacement of the citizen with the consumer, the vote with the debit card.

The neo-liberal agenda is in the ascendancy. It rests upon political arrangements among economic interests that imply the demise of nations, not because nations cannot maintain some semblance of sovereignty, but because they lack the political will to do so. Thus, Canadian leaders buy into the myth-dream. National governments have come up with strategies to commercialize education, deregulate industry, give tax incentives to business, build "innovation clusters" and engage in a "sustained investment branding strategy" that would make Canada competitive in the global market.[110]

Reflecting on Malinowski's insistence that magical and pragmatic methods and modes of understanding are different and refer to different realms of human action and thought, Ralph V. Barrett has identified a major problem with managerial invocations of the myth-dream of transformation. If preliterate people failed to understand the European culture, they at least understood something of magic and its limits; for contemporary college administrators, it seems that the lines are blurred. Barrett explains:

> Unlike Malinowski's natives, educational managers in Ontario's community colleges seem to be insinuating information technology into a set of rituals which confuse magic with the efficient utilization of technique. For example, in a recent convocation speech, one college president, while reminding graduates that computers "still cannot tell you how and when to think, and when to exercise good judgement before you act," went on to say: "Today you take the computer's benefits for granted along with an almost religious faith in its potential for the future. Believe me, I do not think your faith is misplaced." Ultimately and ideologically, the new educational technologies and the epiphany of the paradigm shift can be seen as an exercise in religious faith rather than what Malinowski called "the possession of a considerable store of knowledge, based on experience and fashioned by reason."[111]

Defeating the Defeated

Faith in the future ameliorates disillusionment and defeat today. "It would be nice," says Michael Hammer, "to believe that education and training will bring everyone up to the level required by process-centered jobs. Maybe it's possible, but the prospect of such a dramatic improvement in the American educational system is very doubtful. The problem of what to do with the 'little people' will be with us for some time."[112] Until, that is, they die off, are warehoused in geriatric facilities or incarcerated if their unemployability and consequent poverty lead them to become potential threats to capital, in which case their indigence can simply be criminalized.

Few seers genuinely worry about "little people." Martin speaks condescendingly of those who feel betrayed by an employer who "has had a long-standing policy of employment security" and now reneges on the promise that employee loyalty would be rewarded with job security. In circumstances of unanticipated employment instability, he intones: "The drones panic."[113] New world corporations, however, need not. They can be confident that, if they have successfully brought their other employees into the myth-dream, those other employees – especially when placed in teams where salaries are tied to group productivity – will become "impatient with nonperformers. They [will] expect management to do something about the drones" and, if management is slow off the mark, snitching will quickly trump solidarity.[114]

The language here is instructive. In discussing the social nature of animals, many scientists speak about communication and social organization among mammals, birds, fish and insects. They are reluctant, however, to accord to most animals – chimpanzees and dolphins being among the occasional exceptions – the characteristics of rationality and self-consciousness. It is better, they often say, to think of particular bees, for example, as specialized cells in an organism called a hive rather than as discrete individuals. In the same way, human drones can be discounted in terms of their emotional and economic well-being and denied even the status of individuals within the corporatist structure. In the novelization of Paddy Chayevsky's screenplay *Network*, the corporate myth-dream is splendidly articulated by the character Arthur Jennings:

It's the individual that's finished. It's the single solitary human being who's finished. Because this is no longer a nation of independent individuals. This is a nation of two hundred-odd million transistorized, deodorized, whiter-than-white, steel-belted bodies, totally unnecessary as human beings and replaceable as piston-rods."[115]

Mussolini said somewhere that he regretted labeling his government, his party and his movement "fascist." Such a splendid symbiosis of state and capital ought properly to have been called "corporatism." Perhaps, its time has come.

When Kurt Vonnegut, who began his student career as an undergraduate major in chemistry at Cornell, expressed dissatisfaction with his next academic specialty, physical anthropology, he gave voice to his longing for poetry. His graduate school advisor at the University of Chicago smiled: "How would you like to study poetry which pretends to be scientific?" he asked. "Is such a thing possible?" Vonnegut replied. The kindly advisor shook the callow student's hand. "Welcome," he said, "to cultural anthropology."[116] Vonnegut took heart from Robert Redfield's concept of a folk society, a society in which human relations were personal and not at all instrumental.[117] He died in 2007, still seeking a folk society to join.

The cargo cult is one response to the transformation of folk cultures into rump modernity. Contemporary corporate culture displays what can happen when such societies turn fully into silicon cages. Heartlessness is the visible marker. Funding for prisons becomes preferred to funding for pensions. The mass media teach lessons in the withdrawal of pity. The corporate myth-dream, now manifest in the Free Trade Agreement of the Americas, demands market access to public services and national resources. Restrictive environmental and labour laws are swept aside.

The path to becoming a "Third World planet" is being cleared.

Standing in the way is an e-mail army of indeterminate size and savvy. Its foot soldiers are aware that the U.S.A. is not the completely good society in operation, that history has not ended quite yet, and that the barbed wire barricade in Québec City was a farcical simulacrum of the Maginot Line for corporate myth-dreamers. They understand the strength and determination of their opponents.[118] They know about the failures of their ancestors and are unlikely to call upon them. Those who remember Bob Rae are unforgiving. Even those who have heard of Tommy Douglas have watched Alexa McDonough and shrugged. They are too familiar with repression for dreams, too familiar with deceit for myths. They will sing no songs of innocence.

Yet they may sympathize with the likes of John LeCarré. The old Cold Warrior, who began his sixteen years with MI5 and MI6 by snitching on his fellow students at Oxford, carried on the struggle through his fictional spy, George Smiley, and now, since the collapse of the USSR, is pursuing other themes. A recent novel probes international pharmaceutical companies.[119] It reveals their "pitch-dark underside sustained by corporate cant, hypocrisy, corruption and greed."[120] Assuming he is sincere, he seems to be suffering the angst of those apologists for capitalism who in late middle age finally discover its capacity to do evil; so, he offered this guileless advice to the readers of Britain's *Sunday Telegraph*:

> Perhaps we do indeed need a great new movement, an international, humanitarian movement of decent men and women, that is not doctrinal, not political, not polemical, but gathers up the best in all of us: a Seattle demo without the broken glass.[121]

Alas, broken windows in Seattle have already been

superceded by blown-out brains in Genoa. And, for a time, the anti-globalization movement will focus on organizing against war. But notables such as LeCarré have not let their flirtation with "reform" perish in the rubble of the World Trade Center, nor will they expire as the flames die down in Baghdad. Broad and unambiguous issues are available. So, early in 2003, the creator of Smiley's people had become emboldened. On 15 January, for example, in an "opinion" piece for *The Times* of London, entitled "The United States of America has gone mad," he denounced the "Bush junta" for, among other things, "its shameless favouring of the already-too-rich, its reckless disregard of the world's poor, the ecology and a raft of unilaterally abrogated treaties."

As for the demonstrators, their ignorance of history may mean that they will repeat many, but not necessarily all, of their ancestors' mistakes. Their self-indulgence may protect them from unnecessary compromise. They will be courted but not easily seduced by fifty-something urban and urbane New Democrats to reinvent the not-so-new party by forging a coalition of white whiners and raving "youth."[122] Against hierarchy, leadership and political dogma, they sense "how deeply people are manipulated and manipulate themselves and how social change needs to spring from [the] subjective and inter-subjective level if it is to have lasting significance and proceed democratically." Thus, Ben Agger expresses the challenge of building a bridge from the 1960s to the twenty-first century. He elaborates Herbert Marcuse's argument "that social change needs to begin at home; if it does not do so, if liberty is sacrificed to liberation, then social change merely replaces one authoritarian order with another."[123] It needs to begin but it doesn't need to stay at home, nor to stay at home alone. It needs poetry and humour, but it needs to know that politics is more than performance art. It needs to recall Vonnegut's caution about cruelty of power. In the reflection of the ghastly green light from Basra, it needs to remember Carlo Giuliani, shot dead and run over by the Carabinieri on a street in Genoa. It needs to remember Jean Chrétien's unctuous complaint about "the lack of attention [being paid] to the substance of the summit" and his sanctimonious promise, almost before Giuliani's corpse was cold, that such anarchists would not be allowed to overthrow democracy.[124]

Cargo cults may have been no nobler than corporations, but they were at least more poignant. They deserved better. Critics of corporate culture may learn the virtue of modesty from the cargo cults' failures. They certainly learned that the new millennium was no big deal after all. No New Age ups, no Y2K downs. Western civilization couldn't even decide if it began on 1 January, 2000 or 1 January, 2001, and no one else cared about anything but the fireworks. Now, by deconstructing the corporate myth-dream without succumbing to the temptation to counter it with the internally coherent lunacy of a *fatwa*, they may yet give today's aspirant liberators the best available tools to remake our lives and our world.

Coda

"Myth," writes Frank Zingrone, "has been our time-honoured technique for virtualizing experience."[125] At a time when "humankind lived mythically and deeply," Melanesian myths tried "to synthesize some sort of order out of the whirling flux and make sense of the hidden processes of an overabundant nature."[126] Cargo cults failed because what they sought to mythologize was increasingly unnatural. We are now tenebrously aware of the capacity for what we might anthropomorphize as vengeance by an abused nature; we no longer live deeply; the flaw in the neo-liberal "myth-dream" is the redundancy of virtualizing the already virtual.

NOTES

Portions of this chapter were first presented to the Society for Anthropology in Community Colleges in Toronto (April, 1997).

1. Norman Cohn, *The Pursuit of the Millennium: Revolutionary Messianism in Medieval and Reformation Europe and Its Bearing on Modern Totalitarian Movements*, 2nd ed. (New York: Harper Torchbooks, 1961), p. 319. With only a little difficulty, Ian Baruma shoehorns into the millenarian tradition recent Japanese terrorist groups such as the Red Army Faction in the 1970s and the quasi-Buddhist Aum Shinrikyo cult that released the deadly nerve gas, sarin, in the Tokyo subway in 1995. See "The Japanese Malaise," *The New York Review* (5 July, 2001), pp. 39-41. Of related interest are "up-to-date" apocalyptic beliefs such as those available at www.mahikari.org and described in William Sanborn Pfeiffer, "Mahikari: New Religion and Japanese Popular Culture," *Journal of Popular Culture*, Vol. 34, No. 2, (Fall, 2000). No doubt, when the cycle of rage and revenge subsides, similar analyses will be made of Osama bin Laden and his followers. While it is tempting to note similarities among endemic protests, it is well to remember Eric Hobsbawm's caution against "careless generalization." Millenarian movements such as those of Andalusian peasants no doubt have something in common with, let us say, Melanesian cargo cults: "But," he warns, "it must never be forgotten that the differences may also be great." E. J. Hobsbawm, *Primitive Rebels: Studies in Archaic Forms of Social Movement in the 19th and 20th Centuries* (New York: W. W. Norton, 1965), p. 5. What is less frequently discussed is the imagery of evil that has appeared in American presidential rhetoric. Reagan's evil empire and George W. Bush's (or was it Barbara Frum's brat's?) "axis of evil" derive, according to Joan Didion, from "a kind of reasoning so fragile that it might be based on the promised return of the cargo gods." See: "Fixed Opinions, or the Hinge of History," *The New York Review* (16 January, 2003), p. 55.

2. Lucy Mair, *An Introduction to Social Anthropology*, 2nd ed. (Oxford: Clarendon Press, 1972), p. 253. More bluntly, contemporary anthropology text books occasionally state: "Cargo cults are religious responses to the expansion of the world capitalist economy." Conrad Phillip Kottack, *Mirror for Humanity: A Concise Introduction to Cultural Anthropology*, 3rd ed. (New York: McGraw-Hill, 2003), p. 197.

3. Roger Emerson, "Utopia," in Philip P. Wiener, ed., *Dictionary of the History of Ideas: Studies of Selected Pivotal Ideas*, Vol. 4 (New York: Charles Scribner's Sons, 1973), p. 460.

4. Ernest Tuveson, "Millenarianism," in Philip P. Wiener, ed., *Dictionary of the History of Ideas: Studies of Selected Pivotal Ideas*, Vol. 3 (New York: Charles Scribner's Sons, 1973), p. 225. Some say Marx's use of phrases such as the "dictatorship of the proletariat" prove that he was an incipient totalitarian. If so, a remark that Engels attributed to Marx in a letter to C. Schmidt in 1890 becomes salient: "All I know is that I am not a Marxist."

5. This view was famously put forward by Karl Popper in *The Poverty of Historicism* (London: Routledge & Kegan Paul, 1961) and *The Open Society and Its Enemies* (London: Routledge & Kegan Paul, 1962). It was rebutted by Maurice Cornforth in *The Open Philosophy and The Open Society: A Reply to Dr. Karl Popper's Refutation of Marxism* (New York: International Publishers, 1968).

6. Albert Camus, *The Rebel: An Essay on Man in Revolt* (New York: Vintage, 1956), pp. 105-132, 188-252.

7. While not necessarily accepting his conclusions about "Boasian culturalism," it is hard to dismiss Derek Freeman's critique of Margaret Mead's anthropological research in *Margaret Mead and Samoa: The Making and Unmaking of an Anthropological Myth* (Cambridge MA: Harvard University Press, 1983) and *The Fateful Hoaxing of Margaret Mead: A Historical Analysis of her Samoan Research* (Boulder: Westview Press, 1999).

8. Marvin Harris, *Culture, People, Nature: An Introduction to General Anthropology*, 2nd ed. (New York: Thomas Y. Crowell, 1975), p. 560.

9. *Ibid*. An interesting "take" on Christianity was provided to Lutheran missionary Rolland Hanselmann in 1933. Entering his church, he was confronted by his native helpers and informed that "Jesus Christ gave cargo to the Europeans. Now he wanted to give it to the natives. But the Jews and the missionaries had conspired to keep the cargo for themselves. The Jews had

captured Jesus and were keeping him prisoner in or above Sydney, Australia. But soon Jesus would get free and the cargo would start coming. The poorest would get the most ('the meek shall inherit'). The people stopped work, slaughtered their pigs, burned their gardens and massed in the cemeteries." Marvin Harris, *Cows, Pigs, Wars and Witches: The Riddles of Culture* (New York: Vintage, 1978), p. 121.

10. F.E. Williams, "The Vailala Madness and the Destruction of Native Ceremonies in the Gulf Region," *Territory of Papua Anthropological Reports* 4 (Port Moresby: 1923), quoted in Roger M. Keesing and Felix M. Keesing, *New Perspectives in Cultural Anthropology* (New York: Holt, Rinehart and Winston, 1971), p. 361.

11. Anarcho-communist millenarian movements (often with virulent anti-Semitism at their core) were known in Christendom as well. Cohn, *op. cit.*, pp. 209-236).

12. Annemarie Malefijt, *Religion and Culture: An Introduction to the Anthropology of Religion* (New York: Macmillan, 1968).

13. Marx's comment at the beginning of *The Eighteenth Brumaire of Louis Bonaparte* to the effect that important historical events occur twice, first as tragedy and second as farce, takes on a special poignancy here.

14. Mitchell Smyth, "Island of fire," *The Toronto Star* (4 January, 1997), p. G-9.

15. Marvin Harris, *Cows, Pigs, Wars and Witches*, pp. 116-117.

16. Harris, *Culture, People, Nature*, p. 560.

17. Peter Worsley, *The Trumpet Shall Sound: A Study of "Cargo" Cults in Melanesia* (London: MacGibbon and Key, 1957), p. 12. For additional detailed studies, see Jean Guiart, "John Frum Movement in Tana," *Oceania* 22 (1951), Peter Lawrence, *Road Belong Cargo* (Manchester: Manchester University Press, 1964), and Glyn Cochrane, *Big Men and Cargo Cults* (Oxford: Clarendon Press, 1970).

18. David Aberle, "A Note on Relative Deprivation Theory as Applied to Millenarian and Other Cult Movements," in William A. Lessa and Evon Z. Vogt, eds., *Reader in Comparative Religion: An Anthropological Approach*, 3rd ed. (New York: Harper and Row, 1971), and Bruce M. Knauft, "Cargo Cults and Relational Separation," *Behavior Science Research* 13 (1978).

19. Harris, *Culture, People, Nature*, p. 562.

20. Ralph V. Barrett, "Technoeducation and Teacherless Learning: Learning-Centred Education in Ontario's Colleges," an unpublished paper presented to the Annual Meeting of the Canadian

Sociology and Anthropology Association, St. Catharines (June, 1995), p. 30.

21. Bronislaw Malinowski, *A Scientific Theory of Culture and Other Essays* (New York: Oxford University Press, 1960), p. 198.

22. Bronislaw Malinowski, *Magic, Science and Religion* (Chicago: Waverland Press, 1992), p. 31.

23. Umberto Eco, "Signs of the Times," in Catherine David et al., eds., *Conversations about the End of Time* (London: Penguin, 1999), p. 186.

24. Kenelm Burridge, "Social Implications of Some Tangu Myths," in John Middleton, ed., *Myth and Cosmos: Readings in Mythology and Symbolism* (Garden City: The Natural History Press, 1967), p. 46.

25. *Ibid.*, p. 30.

26. Kenelm Burridge, *Mambu: A Study of Melanesian Cargo Movements and Their Social and Ideological Background* (New York: Harper Torchbooks, 1970), p. 28.

27. *Ibid.*, p. 29.

28. *Ibid.*

29. Marvin Harris, *Cows, Pigs, Wars and Witches*, 117.

30. John McMurtry, in *Unequal Freedoms: The Global Market as an Ethical System* (Aurora: Garamond, 1998), persuasively describes the logic, rhetoric and metaphysics of the corporate myth-dream. "No traditional religion," he says, "has declared more absolutely the universality and necessity of its laws and commandments than the proponents of the global market doctrine." To its adherents, neoliberalism is nothing less than "the revealed design of God." p. 67. Of interest is the assertion by its advocates and analysts that an understanding of America's "civil religion" (its public philosophy couched in broadly theological terms) does not "simply equate it with the Ghost Dance or a Cargo Cult." They do, however, admit that its "purpose is to conserve [a] culture even as it, and the associated establishment, is threatened from within and without." American revitalization movements, however, are "unlike the Ghost Dance . . . and the Cargo Cult" in that the U.S. civil religion "is not . . . futile optimism." It *will* prevail. Robert N. Bellah and Phillip E. Hammond, *Varieties of Civil Religion* (San Francisco: Harper & Row, 1980), pp. 201, 204.

31. Kurt Vonnegut, *Fates Worse than Death: An Autobiographical Collage of the 1980s* (New York: G. P. Putnam's Sons, 1991), p. 131.

32. Despite confused and contested meanings for rapidly mutating

political terms, it is folly to accept the Humpty Dumpty school of political linguistics and to say, with *Masterpiece Theatre* host Russell Baker, that "shop-worn words like 'conservative' and 'liberal' mean whatever anybody saying or writing them want them to mean." See "Mr. Right," *The New York Review* (17 May, 2001), p. 4. If, after all, we cannot at least provisionally define our concepts, we literally won't know what we are talking about. In Europe and decreasingly in Canada the embrace of the market mentality, the denigration of state-supported social investment, the insistence on less government, and a restructured labour force are conflated in the term "neoliberalism." It means a return to eighteenth century notions of a free market unfettered by government intervention in support of the homeless, paved roads or hygiene standards in restaurants. Such political views in the U.S.A. and increasingly in Canada are collectively called "neoconservatism." The terms are regarded here as almost synonymous, except that neoconservatism is often conjoined with socio-religious values reflecting Christian fundamentalism, opposition to multiculturalism and related optional positions including thinly disguised racism, misogyny, and homophobia. For helpful critiques of the neoliberal view that the will of the market is to be preferred to the will of the people, see Noam Chomsky, *Profit Over People: Neoliberalism and Global Order* (New York: Seven Stories Press, 1999), pp. 43-62 and 91-118, and Gary Teeple, *Globalization and the Decline of Social Reform* 2nd, ed. (Aurora: Garamond, 1999), pp. 23-40.

33. Utter devastation may, of course, be unnecessary. Failing education, enfeebled health care, fouled water, and collapsing economic infrastructures are increasingly being attributed to the fetish of privatization in some jurisdictions and effective opposition to neoliberal doctrines may yet emerge. Alternatively, there is no guarantee that "radicalization" will mean a shift to the left. Xenophobic fears rather anger against domestic oppression may lead, for example, to the cryptofascism of the national security state.

34. Kurt Vonnegut, *Player Piano* (New York: Charles Scribner's Sons, 1952).

35. See below, endnote 115.

36. Kurt Vonnegut, "In a Manner that Must Shame God Himself," *Harper's* (November, 1972), reprinted in *Wampeters, Foma and Granfalloons: Opinions* (New York: Dell, 1976), p. 206.

37. In *The Folklore of Capitalism* (New Haven: Yale University

Press, 1937), Thurman Arnold incisively analyzed the fads and foibles of economics and demonstrated that pragmatism need not be a code word for amorality. Therein he recognized, fully two years before the *blitzkrieg*, that "Sweden is a much pleasanter place to live in today than Germany" (p. 333).

38. Cf. the title song from Phil Ochs' album *Tape from California* (A & M: SP4148).

39. Arnold put it nicely when he amusingly sought to explain "how the great sciences of law and economics and the little imaginary people who are supposed to be guided by these sciences affect the daily lives of those who make, distribute and consume our goods." *Ibid.*, p. v.

40. Gardiner Means and Adolph Berle, *The Modern Corporation and Private Property* (New York: Macmillan, 1934).

41. *Salomon* v. *Salomon & Co.* [1897] A.C. 22 at 30 (H.L.), quoted in John A. Yogis, *Canadian Law Dictionary*, 2nd edition (New York: Barron's Educational Series, 1990), p. 54.

42. Quoted in Stewart Brand, "Both Sides of the Necessary Paradox (Conversations with Gregory Bateson)," in *II Cybernetic Frontiers* (New York: Random House, 1974), p. 10.

43. Richard Gwyn, "A prophet in winter," *The Toronto Star* (29 April, 2001), p. D-13.

44. Kari Levitt, *Silent Surrender: The Multinational Corporation in Canada* (Toronto: Macmillan, 1970).

45. Scott Turow, *Pleading Guilty* (New York: Warner Books, 1993), pp. 174-175.

46. Critical theorist Jürgen Habermas has thoughtfully outlined "crisis tendencies in advanced capitalism," in *Legitimation Crisis* (Boston: Beacon Press, 1975).

47. Opportunities always exist for jesters. Abbie Hoffman was one. So might become Jaggi Singh, the young Canadian "anarchist," who was jailed by the authorities in Québec in April, 2001, for offenses apparently related to a plan to toss teddy bears at riot police. See Janet Bagnall, "Justice and Jaggi Singh," *Montreal Gazette* (May 9, 2001). Vonnegut has sensibly cautioned that "clowning doesn't throw off the timing or slow down cruel social machinery. In fact, it usually serves as a lubricant." See "In a Manner that Must Shame God Himself," p. 198.

48. Alexis de Tocqueville, *Democracy in America* (Garden City: Anchor, 1969) p. 692.

49. Douglas famously quoted William Blake's "call to arms against the rise of industrial capitalism." "But," argues Harvard geneticist Richard Lewontin, "what was then a struggle against the

rise of its dominance is now a struggle against its last consolidation in spheres of life that seemed set apart." So, under the leadership of Archer Daniels Midland, Monsanto, Exxon and John Deere, we are forced to witness "the growing dominance of industrial capital in agriculture. It is not Jerusalem that has been built in the green and pleasant land," he says, "it is the dark Satanic mills." See "Genes in the Food!" *The New York Review* (21 June, 2001), p. 84.

50. In the late 1950s, *Tomorrowland* was a monthly segment (along with *Adventureland*, *Fantasyland*, and *Frontierland*) on Disney's weekly CBS television series. Later Sunday evening, *G. E. Theatre*, a weekly drama series was hosted by Ronald Reagan. Wernher von Braun was once thought a "scientist," but Kurt Vonnegut's 1973 interview in *Playboy* reveals that he was not. He may not even have been an official Nazi. Vonnegut says he had "the heartless sort of innocence that would allow a man to invent and build an electric chair – as an act of good citizenship." Von Braun was, of course, an inventor of weapons systems for the Nazis and such people "are not friends of the common man." *Wampeters, Foma and Granfalloons (Opinions)*, pp. 267-268.

51. Coca-Cola's presence remains ominous. A few years ago, journalist Richard Bernstein saw "a banner hanging up in Bodhgaya, the site of the Buddha's enlightenment, saying, 'COCA-COLA WELCOMES HIS HOLINESS THE DALAI LAMA.'" See Pico Iyer, "On the Road," *The New York Review* (17 May, 2001), p. 33.

52. Chile was neo-liberalism's first laboratory experiment (under the bloody hand of General Augusto Pinochet and the tutelage of University of Chicago economist Milton Friedman) in market fascism. For a compelling up-to-date treatment, see Christopher Hitchens' indictment of the role of Henry Kissinger (along with Pepsi, ITT and the Chase Manhattan Bank), *The Trial of Henry Kissinger* (London: Verso, 2001), pp. 55-76. Coca-Cola was involved in similar events in Guatemala two decades earlier. Then, a Coke official listed its enemies as Pepsi-Cola, communists and trade unions, not necessarily in that order.

53. The cross-fertilization of ideas between social and natural studies was once more transparent and openly expressed. Charles Darwin acknowledged his debt to Thomas Malthus and Marx sought (unsuccessfully) to dedicate *Das Kapital* to Darwin. Today, most scientists do not step lightly into unfamiliar terri-

tory. The main exceptions are sociobiologists. Freeman Dyson, for instance, insists that his concepts "can be transferred without difficulty from a molecular context to ecological, economic and cultural contexts" and, while declaring of a recent volume that he did "not intend [his] book to be a manifesto in defense of free enterprise," just couldn't seem to help himself. See *Origins of Life*, 2nd edition (Cambridge: Cambridge University Press, 1999), pp. 85-86. Dyson remains in the thrall of Richard Dawkins who, Dyson breathlessly affirms, had earlier "brilliantly explored the relationship between the genetic evolution of biological species and the cultural evolution of human societies." *Ibid.*, p. 87. Dawkins offers the reductionist opinion that genes "have created us body and mind" in *The Selfish Gene* (New York: Oxford University Press, 1976), p. 21. Richard Lewontin has recently added to the debate in *It Ain't Necessarily So: The Dream of the Human Genome and Other Illusions* (New York: New York Review Books, 2001).

54. Just as Jesus ought not to be held wholly accountable for seventeenth-century witch burnings, nor Marx for twentieth-century Gulags, so Adam Smith does not deserve all the blame for the misanthropy that is carried on in his name. Free enterprise, after all, was potentially egalitarian and once constituted a revolutionary alternative to mercantilism. As McMurtry reminds us, disciples such as Milton Friedman have seriously distorted Smith's views. He was, after all, a professor of *moral* philosophy and author of the hit of the 1757 publishing year, *The Theory of Moral Sentiments*. He endorsed universal public education and agreed with the principle of self-interest only with limitations and only insofar as it promoted the public good. He regarded private firms as an injustice against the poor, rejecting corporations as "a lamentable exception to the free market system." McMurtry, *op. cit.*, pp. 132-139.

55. Edmund Burke, *Reflections on the Revolution in France* (Chicago: Henry Regnery, 1962), p. 112.

56. Karl Marx and Friedrich Engels, *The Communist Manifesto* (New York: Appleton-Century-Crofts, 1955), pp. 12-13.

57. Warren G. Bennis and Michael Mische, *The 21st Century Organization: Reinventing Through Reengineering* (San Diego: Pfeiffer, 1995), p. 20.

58. The classic critique of Taylorism is Harry Braverman, *Labor and Monopoly Capital: The Degradation of Work in the Twentieth Century* (New York: Monthly Review Press, 1974), pp. 85-138. A Canadian variant is James W. Rinehart, *The Tyranny of Work:*

Alienation and the Labour Process, 3rd ed. (Toronto: Harcourt Brace, 1996). Supporters of Taylorism include management guru Peter F. Drucker, who reminds us that "the German General Staff, having lost the First World War, applied Taylor's Scientific Management to the job of the soldier and to military training. This," he says, "enabled Hitler to create a superb fighting machine in the six short years between his coming to power and 1939." As for Taylor's critics, Drucker dismisses them as mere "craft unions" that were foolishly preoccupied with "the *mystique* of craft skill." Peter F. Drucker, *Management Challenges for the 21st Century* (New York: HarperBusiness, 1999), pp. 140, 138.

59. Braverman, *op. cit.*, p. 67.

60. Most psychotherapy equates mental health with compliance with social norms, adaptation to social circumstances and integration into established social institutions. All else is "abnormal" and therefore in need of treatment. Even self-identified "radical" psychologists rarely threaten power relations and thus emerge as closet supporters of dominant ideologies, as Russell Jacoby has explained in *Social Amnesia: A Critique of Conformist Psychology from Adler to Laing* (Boston: Beacon, 1975). Conversely, the few genuinely radical economists usually pay dearly for the privilege of criticism.

61. Representative is Robert A. Baron, *Behavior in Organizations: Understanding and Managing the Human Side of Work* (Boston: Allyn and Bacon, 1983). The text is laced with special inserts "From the Manager's Perspective" on such topics as "Using Operant Conditioning: A Practical Guide," "Intrinsic Motivation: When Does Pay Lower Motivation?" and "Organizational Politics: Some General Strategies for Seizing, Holding and Using Power."

62. The phrase is borrowed from Geoff Pervere's insightful article on the legacy of punk rock, "No future?" *The Toronto Star* (2 June, 2001), p. J-15.

63. Interest in diverse Japanese business practices have come, gone and come again. See, for example, Eleanor D. Glor, "Towards Understanding the Innovation Process in Canadian Governments," an unpublished paper presented at the 1997 Roundtable of the International Institute of Administrative Studies (Québec City). Her views on Ikujiro Nonaka and Hirotaka Takouchi, *The Knowledge-Creating Company: How Japanese Companies Create the Dynamic of Innovation* (New York: Oxford University Press, 1995) are especially noteworthy.

64. Michael Crichton, *Rising Sun* (New York: Knopf, 1992). William S. Ouchi, *Theory Z: How American Business Can Meet the Japanese Challenge* (Reading: Addison-Wesley, 1981).

65. For revealing insights into IBM's corporate history and ethics, see Edwin Black, *IBM and the Holocaust: The Strategic Alliance between Nazi Germany and America's Most Powerful Corporation* (New York: Crown Publishers, 2001).

66. Warren G. Bennis, "Beyond Bureaucracy," in Warren G. Bennis and Philip E. Slater, *The Temporary Society* (New York: Harper Colophon, 1968), pp. 58-59. Those disconcerted by the convergence of corporations and the counter-culture might enjoy the reflections of molecular geneticist Gunther S. Stent who observed that "by the 1960s, the beatniks had faded from view, not because they had actually disappeared but because their attitudes and styles had become commonplace." See *Paradoxes of Progress* (San Francisco: W. H. Freeman, 1976), p. 17. The beats' antipathy to careerism was amplified by human resource managers who brought itinerant amateurism from a marginal option to a corporate priority, thus proving the wisdom of the admonition to be careful what you wish for, lest your wish be granted.

67. *Ibid.*, p. 75.

68. Philip E. Slater, "Some Social Consequences of Temporary Systems," in Bennis and Slater, *op. cit.*, p. 77.

69. "Testimony before the Industrial Relations Commission," April, 1914, in Keith Davis and John W. Newstrom, eds., *Organizational Behavior: Readings and Exercises*, 6th edition (New York: McGraw-Hill, 1981), p. 38.

70. Western Electric Company, "The Hawthorne Studies 1924/1974: A Synopsis," *Industrial Engineering* (November, 1974), p. 15.

71. Bret Easton Ellis, *American Psycho* (New York: Vintage, 1991). A focus of nervous debate about censorship for some years, this singularly unpleasant novel satirized the lifestyle of a young stockbroker-cum-serial killer. It was partly responsible for the dismissal of at least one popular but untenured college professor who included it in his curriculum.

72. John L. Mariotti, *The Power of Partnerships: The Next Step Beyond TQM, Reengineering and Lean Production* (Cambridge MA: Blackwell, 1996). Mariotti wanted management to enter collaborative relationships with unions. While admitting that dealing with a union that may have had "prior adversary relations" with management "alters some of the 'rules,'" he insisted that "it does not (or should not) alter the basic ones – trust,

character, active communications, common goals, and so
forth." The basic problem, as he defined it, "is that some union
leaders may feel threatened and become obstacles to the partnership." *Ibid.* p. 123-124. An instructive case study of Magma
Metals, a subsidiary of Magma Copper Company, which was
created as a laboratory for a new cooperative approach to man-
agement-labour relations, can be found in Douglas K. Smith,
*Taking Charge of Change: 10 Principles for Managing People and
Performance* (Reading: Addison-Wesley, 1995).

73. James Martin, *The Great Transition: Using the Seven Disciplines
of Enterprise Engineering to Align People, Technology and
Strategy* (New York: American Management Association,
1995), p. 449. Here, as ever, language matters. Management
calls collective bargaining agreements "union contracts," imply-
ing that managers should be exempt from responsibility for creating the conditions that compel workers to defend themselves
and for being willing signatories to their agreements.

74. Warren G. Bennis, *Why Leaders Can't Lead: The Unconscious
Conspiracy Continues* (San Francisco: Jossey-Bass, 1990), p. 87.

75. Gary Johns, *Organizational Behavior: Understanding Life at
Work* (Glenview: Scott Foresman, 1983), p. 501.

76. Martin Nicolaus, "Remarks at the ASA Convention," mimeo
(Boston, 1968), pp. 2-3.

77. Globalization, of course, is merely a fresh name for mercantilism, colonialism and imperialism. It differs structurally from earlier versions mainly in terms of the role of the state. In the eighteenth century, for example, the British East India Company colluded with the British government and the Dutch East India
Company colluded with the Dutch government in competition
for trade with Asia. The companies got rich and the governments got proud. When, however, governments showed themselves unwilling to repress democratic reforms, unable to throt-
tle demands for public spending on social investment, and incapable of stifling *all* the aspirations of common citizens, international corporations decided to downsize governments and go it
almost alone. Quite apart from any "war on terrorism," even the
end of the Cold War did not bring a "peace dividend" as military
spending continued to provide enormous private sector profits.
Like domestic police forces and private security services, armies
are recognized as "costs of doing business." Other expenditures
in support of the common weal (debt reduction or the maintenance, to say nothing of the expansion, of social investment)
have daunting corporate obstacles to overcome.

78. Bennis and Mische, *op. cit.*, pp. 23-25.

79. Robert H. Miles, *Corporate Comeback: The Story of Renewal and Transformation at National Semiconductor* (San Francisco: Jossey-Bass, 1997), p. 388.

80. Martin, *op. cit.*, pp. 446-447.

81. *Ibid.*, p. 447.

82. Quoted in *ibid.*, p. 153.

83. *Ibid.*, p. 11.

84. David K. Carr and Henry J. Johansson, *Best Practices in Reengineering: What Works and What Doesn't in the Reengineering Process* (New York: McGraw-Hill, 1995), p. 40.

85. *Ibid.*, p. 38.

86. See Joseph Fletcher, *Situation Ethics: The New Morality* (Philadelphia: Westminster Press, 1966) and Harvey Cox, ed., *The Situation Ethics Debate* (Philadelphia: Westminster Press, 1968). For a refreshingly "retro" look at the evolution of moral thinking that has witnessed the criteria of "wrong" behaviour shift from religious to legal to psychological domains now culminating in "collective irresponsibility," see Karl Menninger, *Whatever Became of Sin?* (New York: Hawthorn, 1973).

87. The inspiration for this exercise is generally agreed to be the case of *U.S. v. Holmes, 26 Fed. Cas. No. 360*, in which a crewman on the ship *William Brown* was tried for murder in the deaths of a number of passengers whom he forced out of a lifeboat that was badly overcrowded and foundering in heavy seas. See William A. Rutter, *Criminal Law* (New York: Harcourt Brace Jovanovich, 1976) sections 213-218.

88. John P. Kotter, "Leading Change: Why Transformation Efforts Fail," in James Champy and Nitin Nohria, eds., *Fast Forward: The Best Ideas on Managing Business Change* (Boston: Harvard Business School Press, 1996), p. 89. The art of crisis creation also flourishes in government. In the neo-liberal regime of Premier Mike Harris in Ontario, education minister John Snobelen gained brief infamy for unknowingly speaking into a "live" microphone about the importance of manufacturing a crisis in education in order to solve it. His "ramblings about power and change and declarations and leadership [revealed] a messianic world in which a vision divorced from the bother of consulting voters and teachers and parents and ordinary folk is simply imposed by strong leaders from above." Jim Coyle, "Book unmasks the Harrisite modus operandi," *The Toronto Star* (29 May, 2001), p. B-1, and Ruth Cohen, *Alien Invasion* (Toronto: Insomniac Press, 2001).

89. H. H. Gerth and C. Wright Mills, eds., *From Max Weber: Essays in Sociology* (New York: Oxford University Press, 1958), pp. 245-264.

90. Max Weber, *The Protestant Ethic and the Spirit of Capitalism* (New York: Charles Scribner's Sons, 1958), p. 182.

91. Kotter, *op. cit.*, pp. 92-93. See also, Drucker, *op. cit.*, pp. 72-93.

92. Linda McQuaig thus summarized Angell's comments on the CBC radio program, *Sunday Morning* (1 December, 1996) in *The Cult of Impotence: Selling the Myth of Powerlessness in the Global Economy* (Toronto: Viking, 1998), p. 12.

93. *Ibid.*, pp. 46, 62.

94. Dalton Camp, "Ivy league rebellion leaves room for hope," *The Toronto Star* (6 May, 2001), p. A-13.

95. Recent antidotes to this ideological epidemic include Maude Barlow and Tony Clarke, *Global Showdown: How the New Activists Are Fighting Global Corporate Rule* (Toronto: Stoddart, 2001), David C. Korten, *When Corporations Rule the World,* second edition (Bloomfield CT: Kumarian Press, 2001), and Naomi Klein's iconic *No Logo: Taking Aim at the Brand Bullies* (Toronto: Knopf, 2000).

96. Douglas Smith, *op. cit.*, p. 283.

97. Michael Hammer, *Beyond Reengineering: How the Process-Centered Organization Is Changing Our Work and Our Lives* (New York: HarperBusiness, 1996), p. 105.

98. Drucker, *op. cit.*, p. 74.

99. Nicholas Von Hoffman, *Capitalist Fools: Tales of American Business from Carnegie to Forbes to the Milken Gang* (New York: Doubleday, 1992), pp. 191-192.

100. Francis Fukayama, in *The End of History and the Last Man* (New York: Free Press, 1992), claims that, with the Soviet Union's collapse, history's main battles have been fought and won. So humanity can now get on with the business of business. Sociologists S. M. Lipset and Daniel Bell said the same forty years ago. For Lipset there was no need to seek the "good society," because the U.S.A. was "the good society in operation." See *Political Man: The Social Bases of Politics* (Garden City: Doubleday, 1960), p. 403. Bell likewise dismissed normative political beliefs in *The End of Ideology: On the Exhaustion of Political Ideas in the Fifties* (New York: Free Press, 1960). In *The Coming of Post-Industrial Society* (New York: Basic Books, 1973), he foretold the "subordination of the corporation," and a shift from "market rationality" to a "communal ethic in busi-

ness," (p. 298). Firms, he said, were self-financing through profits and relied less on equity capital, so "ownership is simply a legal fiction." Thus, he explained, since "private enterprise" institutions are no longer "private property" institutions, they would become more socially responsible. As for workers, he thought it "politically and morally unthinkable that their lives should be at the mercy of a financial speculator" (p. 294). In fact, global corporations are arbiters of political judgement, usurpers of national sovereignty and, in Richard Gwyn's phrase, "stateless legislators." See *Nationalism without Walls: The Unbearable Lightness of Being Canadian* (Toronto: McClelland and Stewart, 1995).

101. Lewis Lapham, on the CBC Newsworld television program, *Hot Type* (16 April, 2001).

102. Mairuth Sarsfield, on the CBC Newsworld television program, *The Editors* (16 April, 2001).

103. Lester C. Thurlow, *The Future of Capitalism: How Today's Economic Forces Shape Tomorrow's World* (New York: William Morrow, 1996), p. 310. Similarly, social democratic apostate Bob Rae argues in *The Three Questions* (Toronto: Viking, 1998) that there is no alternative to capitalism and that the only remaining issue about which citizens may earnestly dither is what kind of capitalism we are to have.

104. Martin, *op. cit.*, p. 186.

105. The tale is told by Pulitzer Prize-winning journalist Kurt Eichenwald, *The Informant: A True Story* (New York: Broadway Books, 2000).

106. Tyler Hamilton, "Nortel cuts 10,000 jobs, projects record losses," *The Toronto Star* (16 June, 2001), pp. A-1, A-34. Earlier myth-dreamer Susan Goldberg had reported that Nortel was "the quintessential model for how Canadian companies should go global." See *Global Pursuit: Canadian Business Strategies for Winning in the Borderless World* (Toronto: McGraw-Hill, 1991), p. 100. In 2002, Nortel stocks were under $1.00 a share but in early 2003, they had rallied to reach over $3.00. Cried the dreamers: "Excelsior!"

107. The Russian Lada was, for a time, noteworthy. Italian by design and made with parts from many Soviet republics, these cars were assembled in Nova Scotia, thus enabling dealers to claim (however fatuously) that they were 100% Canadian vehicles.

108. Microsoft's ongoing troubles with U.S. anti-trust laws as well as the failures of some corporate mergers of U.S. airlines and Canadian banks are examples of pot-holes on the road to corpo-

rate heaven. Road repair, however, is underway as the U.S. exempts dividends from taxation, allowing Bill Gates to pocket over $100 million in 2003, as a result of his company's first-ever dividend payment. Ben Berkowitz, "Gates to reap gains from Microsoft dividend," *The Toronto Star* (18 January, 2003), p. F-5.

109. International relations scholar Richard Rosencrance's presents the corporate myth-dream in the form of prophecy in *The Rise of the Virtual State: Wealth and Power in the Coming Century* (New York: Basic Books, 1999).

110. Some peeps of protest can be heard. In April, 2001, for instance, Mexican President Vincente Fox hinted that foreign aid as well as free trade was important to Third World countries. Such atavisms are allowed if they are mainly for domestic consumption. If, however, such remarks are sincere, there are ample precedents as to the fate of national leaders who stand in the way of progress. Canada, on the contrary, has launched an innovation strategy that relies on ideas promoted by such organizations as the Business Council on National Issues and has been developed by a unique "partnership" among Industry Canada, Human Resources Development Canada and the private research organization, The Conference Board of Canada. See, for example, *Achieving Excellence: Investing in People, Knowledge and Opportunity* (Ottawa: Government of Canada, 2002).

111. Barrett, *op. cit.*, pp. 30-31.

112. Hammer, *op. cit.*, p. 260.

113. Martin, *op. cit.*, p. 446.

114. *Ibid.*, p. 447.

115. Sam Hedrin, *Network* (New York: Pocket Books, 1976), p. 133. Earlier, Kurt Vonnegut said similar things in *Player Piano*. A GE alumnus like Ronald Reagan, Vonnegut imagined a revolt of the drones inspired by the Ghost Dance religion, the most direct Native American analog to the cargo cults. The Ghost Dance originated near the California-Nevada border at the time of the completion of the Union Pacific Railroad. In 1869, a Paiute prophet named Wodziwob foretold the return of the dead on an immense train, the expulsion of the whites who would leave their material goods behind, and the restoration of Indian lands. Like the cargo cults, this response to colonialism promised an earthly paradise in which the Great Spirit would join the Indians, "all happy and forever young." To hasten the realization of the myth-dream, the Indians were encouraged to perform ritual

dances and songs that had come to Wodziwob in his visions, and to wear magical ghost shirts. Some cultists attempted military insurrection and were crushed. In 1889, the cult was revived by the prophet Wovoka. Designs that Wovoka saw in visions were painted on the ghost shirts making them, some believed, bullet-proof. The Ghost Dance prophecy spread to many tribes that sent emissaries to learn the Ghost Dance rituals from Wovoka. The Sioux, who had defeated Custer in 1876, embraced a radical version of the myth-dream. Having been conquered, starved and relocated to nonproductive agricultural lands, their conditions were so appalling that a vision promising the disappearance of their oppressors and the return of traditional ways was extremely appealing. It did not, however, prevent the capture and killing of the Sioux leader Sitting Bull nor the final failure of the myth-dream. On 29 December, 1890, Custer's old unit, the Seventh Cavalry, massacred about 350 men, women and children at Wounded Knee, South Dakota. See J. Mooney, *The Ghost Dance Religion*, Bureau of American Ethnology, Annual Report 14 (Washington: U.S.A. Government Printing Office, 1896) and Alice Beck Kehoe, *The Ghost Dance: Ethnohistory and Revitalization* (Fort Worth: Holt, Rinehart & Winston, 1989). Those interested will also find clear parallels to cargo cults in the Rastafarian religion of Jamaica. See William F. Lewis, *Soul Rebels: The Rastafari* (Prospect Heights IL: Waveland, 1993).

116. Kurt Vonnegut, "Address to the National Institute of Arts and Letters, 1971," in *Wampeters, Foma and Granfalloons (Opinions)*, pp. 173-182.

117. Robert Redfield, "The Folk Society," *American Journal of Sociology*, Vol. 52, No. 2 (January, 1947), pp. 293-308. According to Redfield, in contrast to modern societies "a folk society exhibits culture to the very highest degree." Writes Redfield: "A culture is an organization or integration of conventional understandings." Culture is an "integrated whole [which] provides for all the recurrent needs of the individual from birth to death and of the society through the seasons." *Ibid.*, p. 298. By this reckoning, modern societies (to say nothing of corporations) might be unable to boast of having a culture at all.

118. It is a strength that some global enthusiasts want to expand. Convinced that American isolationism is indefensible and that Third World poverty and tyranny result from too little Westernization not too much, analysts like Oxford professor

Niall Ferguson think that greater U.S. hegemony will promote prosperity not by introducing democracy but by broadening the rule of law. The case is made in *The Cash Nexus: Money and Power in the Modern World 1700-2000* (New York: Basic Books, 2001). Ferguson's sense of irony was intact when he mocked "a summit about integrating trade in the Americas" decorated with "little Quebecois flags to make the point that [it] is 'a northern Latino' nation." Quoted in Rick McGinnis, "Globalization and Its Discontents," *eye* (17 May, 2001), p. 67.

119. John LeCarré, *The Constant Gardener* (New York: Scribner's, 2001). More recently, an Internet document, attributed to LeCarré, is more explicit: "Without bin Laden, the Bush junta would still be trying to explain such tricky matters as how it came to be elected in the first place; Enron; its shameless favouring of the already-too-rich; its reckless disregard for the world's poor, the ecology and a raft of unilaterally abrogated international treaties."

120. Quoted in Hilary Mantel, "The Devil's Playground," *The New York Review* (19 July, 2001), pp. 23-24.

121. *Ibid.*, p. 20.

122. Friends of Judy Rebick, who are accused of unaccountably imagining they could open a web site *and* keep their plans secret, are said to have winced when the *Globe and Mail* scooped the story with a front-page headline reading: "Rebels Aim to Dissolve NDP, Form New Party." See Glenn Wheeler, "Out in left field," *Now* (14 June, 2001), p. 29. As Wheeler also points out, the only people who use the word "youth" aren't.

123. Ben Agger, *Critical Social Theories: An Introduction* (Boulder: Westview Press, 1998), p. 31. See also Herbert Marcuse, *An Essay on Liberation* (Boston: Beacon Press, 1969

124. Les Whittington, "Protester shot dead in Genoa in bloodiest anti-summit riot," *The Toronto Star* (21 July, 2001), p. A-1.

125. Frank Zingrone, *The Media Symplex* (Toronto: Stoddart, 2001), p. 55.

126. *Ibid.*, p. 57.

CONTRIBUTORS

William Anselmi grew up in Orvieto, Umbria. He's now a resident in Edmonton, Alberta. He has published with Kosta Gouliamos, *Mediating Culture* and *Elusive Margins* (Guernica Editions). He's presently working on a book, *Towards a Poetics of Displaced Literature: A Collection of Essays on Mary Melfi* (Guernica Editions) that will appear shortly. Dr. Anselmi is an Associate Professor in the MLCS department, University of Alberta. He is the producer and co-host at CJSR of Radio Sirena.

Osvaldo Croci teaches International Politics and International Political Economy at Memorial University of Newfoundland. His main areas of research are transatlantic relations and Italian foreign policy.

Howard A. Doughty has been with Seneca College since 1969. He currently teaches Cultural Anthropology and Philosophy in the Faculty of Applied Arts and Health Sciences at its campus in King City, Ontario, and is a shop steward for the Ontario Public Service Employees Union, Local 560. Formerly editor of *Bridges: Explorations in Science, Technology and Society* (1986-1991) and *The College Quarterly* (1992-1997), he has been Book Review Editor of *The Innovation Journal* since 1998.

Eva C. Karpinski is a doctoral candidate in Women's Studies at York University in Toronto. Her research interests include feminist theory, women's autobiography, translation studies, ethnic-immigrant writing, utopianism, and postmodernist fiction. She has published articles on John Barth, Joseph Skvorecky, Thomas Pynchon, Angela Carter, Mary Melfi, and Eva Hoffman. She has edited a Canadian multicultural anthology, *Pens of Many Colours* (third edition).

Robin Mathews has taught Canadian Literature and Canadian Studies at Carleton University in Ottawa, Ontario, and at Simon Fraser University in Burnaby, British Columbia. He has produced several books of cultural and literary criticism, among which is *Treason Of The Intellectuals: English Canada in The Post-Modern Period* (Voyageur Publishing, 1995). He also has written numerous essays for many journals on Canadian literature, culture, and society. At the same time, Robin Mathews has published books of poetry and his short stories have appeared in various magazines. A driving force in the Canadian nationalist movement since the 1960s, he continues to work for an authentic Canadian voice in academic and public life.

Marino Tuzi has a Ph.D. in English Literature, with a specialization in Canadian Literature and minority writing from York University. He has produced a book of literary criticism on minority writing in Canada, *The Power Of Allegiances*, published by Guernica Editions. He also has published essays on minority writing in Canada and on topics related to minority experience and Canadian society in various journals and books of essay collections. He teaches Canadian Literature and Canadian Studies at Seneca College in King City, Ontario.